CU00921886

Dear Ailsa, Sometimes I wonder wh[c]
caught us both—a most unlikely frien[d]
find an echo in a far off Irish village som[e]
of old Donegal. Or am I allowing that
mine too much slack?

This is the story of an unlikely friendship.

When priest and Sydneysider Tony Doherty emailed Melbourne-based writer and performer Ailsa Piper to say how much he had enjoyed her latest book, he was met with a swift reply from a similarly enquiring mind. Soon emails were flying back and forth and back again. They exchanged stories of their experiences as sweaty pilgrims and dissected dinner party menus. They shared their delight in Mary Oliver's poetry and wrestled with what it means to love and to grieve. This energetic exchange of words, questions and ideas grew into an unexpected but treasured friendship.

Collected here is that correspondence, brimming with empathy, humour and a fierce curiosity about each other and the worlds, shoes and histories that they inhabit. Described by one reader as 'a demonstration of how to have a conversation and a friendship', *The Attachment* is an intriguing, entertaining and moving celebration of family, faith, connection—even the correct time of day to enjoy rhubarb.

Dear Tony, Funny how our ears tune in to things. How our priorities shift based on who and what we know. How we come to care about such abstract or remote things through the experience of another. Lovely, somehow, but so serendipitous. All the other things we might care about. All that we might have missed had we not stopped to care for this person. I'm glad we stopped for each other.

Praise for *The Attachment*

'Unless your heart is made of stone, *The Attachment* will stir in you a deep yearning for connection, for quiet communion, for conversation, for intimacy, for wisdom, for faith, for love . . . for a joyful engagement with life itself. It is the chronicle of an unlikely but beautiful friendship that will inspire you to value your own friendships more highly, and to nurture them more carefully.' **Hugh Mackay, author of *Beyond Belief***

'*The Attachment* captures the intoxication of being swept into a new and deeply nourishing friendship. It fizzes with joy and humour, wrestles with agonising questions, always anchored in compassion and wisdom.' **Debra Oswald, author of *Useful***

'From the first seed of recognition, the feverish exchange of ideas and confidences, to a deep and abiding appreciation, *The Attachment* is a candid, illuminating journey into the heart of a profound and unexpected friendship, and a testament to the art of correspondence.' **Kat Stewart, actor**

'*The Attachment* made me want to notice my world, love my world, shape it into words. It is a book about friendship but more than that, these two letter-writers—these unlikely friends—are mature enough to know the value of the moment, the value of friendship, how precious and fleeting life is. Both writers are warm, curious, playful, and their letters are rich and full of story and connection. I was moved, and

surprised, and completed the book in a veil of tears. Because I felt the mystery behind the letters, I felt the presence of death and darkness in so much light, and life. Both authors are vulnerable travellers, questioning their corresponding worlds, appreciating the good, challenging the bad, the wrong. I appreciated the way Ailsa and Tony were open about their differences. I loved it that both writers ask What is God, What is life and What do we live for? And in the very next sentence they will share the weather, breakfast, the chores of the day. The book enriched me, and inspired me. It felt to me full of dignity and searching.'
Sofie Laguna, Miles Franklin award-winning author of *The Eye of the Sheep*

'*The Attachment* is a beautifully written, *soulful* book about friendship and what really matters in this life. To read it is to be present at the unfurling of a tender friendship between two thoughtful, compassionate humans, and like all the best collections of letters it's also a discursive wander through life's big questions. It will make you grateful for what you have, while urging you to seize the day with the people you love. It made me think about atonement, and responsibility, and freedom; memory, and poetry, and how to farewell the dying. *The Attachment* is a hymn to paying attention, to walking and swimming and to the deeply consoling role of ritual in our lives. It will make you want to write letters: *good* ones. I will read this book again and again.'
Charlotte Wood, Stella Prize-winning author of *The Natural Way of Things*

THE ATTACHMENT

LETTERS FROM A MOST UNLIKELY FRIENDSHIP

Ailsa Piper

Tony Doherty

ALLEN&UNWIN

SYDNEY · MELBOURNE · AUCKLAND · LONDON

First published in 2017

Allen & Unwin
83 Alexander Street
Crows Nest NSW 2065
Australia
Phone: (61 2) 8425 0100
Email: info@allenandunwin.com
Web: www.allenandunwin.com

Cataloguing-in-Publication details are available
from the National Library of Australia
www.trove.nla.gov.au

ISBN 978 1 76029 468 7

Internal design by Romina Panetta
Set in 11.5/19.5 pt Haboro and 12/19.5 Hoefler Text by Midland Typesetters, Australia
Printed and bound in Australia by Griffin Press

10 9 8 7 6 5

FOR OUR FAMILIES.
YOU BEGAN THE CONVERSATION.

DEAR READER,

This is the story of an unlikely friendship.

My name is Ailsa Piper. I'm a 57-year-old writer, walker, teacher, theatre director and, once upon a time, actress. The other half of 'us' is an 82-year-old swimmer, walker, educator and priest called Tony Doherty.

Friends used to look at me sideways when I mentioned him.

'Tony? Is he your priest mate?'

They're used to the idea now, but it took a while. I'm not a churchgoer and I don't seek conversion, so I wasn't on the lookout for a conversation with a cleric. I grew up kind-of Catholic, but if I had to define myself in terms of

I

belief systems I would perhaps call myself an agnostic with pantheistic leanings–a fence-sitter!

I'm prepared to cop such sledging on the chin. I'm content to be undecided, and live comfortably with the idea that all we have is uncertainty. As a lover of ritual and things mystical or mysterious, I've often yearned for belief, but I've never been able to make that leap. So a friendship with a priest took me by surprise.

How did it happen?

Well, at Easter 2012, Tony was given a copy of my book *Sinning Across Spain,* by a mutual friend. As Tony tells it, the last thing he wanted at Easter (peak season for a priest) was a book about sins, but he read it and three weeks later, he wrote to me.

That book is an account of a 1300-kilometre walk I took on a pilgrim road in Spain, shouldering the sins of friends, colleagues and strangers. Back in 2010, I was doing some research for a play I was adapting, when I found an intriguing little piece of information. It stated that in medieval times, a person could be paid to carry the sins of another to a holy place. On arrival, the stay-at-home received absolution, while the walker got to keep any blisters they'd earned on the way.

Before I could think about it I put out a call. 'Pilgrim seeks sinners for mutually beneficial arrangement,' I wrote. It went viral! People donated sins to me. They wrote to me of their shame and regret. A swag of 'sinners' confessed and I carried, wanting to test whether healing, or transformation, might result. That was the premise of the story Tony read over Easter. So I guess our friendship began with sin; with 'disclosure'–a word Tony uses a lot.

Disclosure characterised our exchanges. That first email of Tony's was answered immediately by me, and the correspondence grew like topsy. Few boundaries constrained our exchanges, even though we are more easily defined by our differences than our similarities. We endeavoured to listen with care and respect. Tony and I share a love of conversation and a wish to find common ground–if not agreement–on everything from afterlife to walking to the best licorice allsorts. As a result, there were surprises, laughter and, occasionally, tears. Best of all, though, a friendship began.

Whenever I spoke about our letters, people frequently expressed longing at the possibility of a thoughtful pen-pal and, even more often, curiosity about the content of our correspondence. What was this 'odd couple' finding to say to each other? At a time when much of the talk between people from opposite sides of fences is so polarised, we thought we might see if our dialogue could be of interest. (Not that we oppose each other in everything, but it must be said that Tony's insistence on rugby as football offends my AFL sensibilities.) We decided to use our correspond-ence as the basis of a book.

We spent months wrangling, in person and via email, trying to develop our ideas and playing with form. We wrote dialogues, trying to articulate the sorts of conver-sations we had. We took turns writing essays about what we felt mattered. We wrote and re-wrote, slogged and got bogged. We put the text down for over a year, thinking it would never see the light of day.

Then, I was awarded a writing residency at Bundanon, a property gifted to the nation by the artist Arthur Boyd. On the banks of the Shoalhaven River, it's a place of natural beauty and silence, two things that ignite my imagination and work ethic. One day, unable to make headway with another project, I decided to have a look at our manuscript.

I read and read, all day and into the night, as wombats snuffled and growled under the floorboards. I couldn't put it down. I was taken back to the beginning of our correspondence, and marvelled at how far we had come. It's easy to forget beginnings when you're a long way down the track. This is something I know from walking. The first steps of an epic hike are rarely as memorable as the last, and yet they should be. They're built on hope and possibility, two things without which our days are bleak.

Not stopping to draw breath, I cut 30,000 words, paring the manuscript back to nothing but our early letters. I sent the text to Tony, saying I thought everything else we had written was too pretentious or self-conscious, and didn't sound like us at all. I suggested we interpolate some letters to a Reader–to you–and leave it at that. Tony agreed immediately. Whenever that rare occurrence takes place, I figure we must be on the right track!

And so, dear Reader, you are holding in your hands a piece of two lives. It might seem a little strange to give you words that were not intended for publication, but they are a heartfelt offering, and they are us–for better and, sometimes, very much for worse!

These letters were the beginning of a friendship that supported me through some of the darkest and most frightening days of my life. For that—and for Tony—I am grateful. Every day.

I wish for you Tony's customary sign-off: happy days. It's easy to write those words, but to be able to recognise a happy day, and to embrace it and be grateful for it, may be one of the most important things we can do. Here's to living in happy days.

Ailsa

DEAR READER,

Few friends would argue with the proposition that I talk a bit. Lucky, really—in my job you're expected to talk *a lot*. What I like most, however, is just easy conversation—a little unhurried time for a meal, a lazy hour in a pub, stories that cause belly laughs and the odd tear.

Sadly, a lot of my talking is monologue. A pulpit homily doesn't allow for much genuine feedback. At its best, conversation dances—opening up, exploring connections, sharing stories, earthy humour, at times a little weep. Even wracking sobs. The letters that follow were the beginning of a conversation that continues to unfold ...

My name is Tony Doherty. Last big one, birthday that is, was 82. Should have retired years ago, of course, but much of my work is simply fun. Almost all of it carries a quiet sense of deep satisfaction, even in the damaged Church we have today.

As a Catholic priest who had been standing still in pulpits for over five decades, a few years ago I felt this baffling impulse to walk a 350-kilometre section of the famous Camino Frances, an ancient pilgrim road in northern Spain that leads from the Pyrenees mountains to Santiago de Compostela. I reached the cathedral at Santiago on the day of my 75th birthday—rather chuffed, really.

On the road, I'd listened to deeply human stories— stories that were golden. Sometimes they were in a language not my own, but still I understood their meaning. A little, at least. The irony is, however, that one of my richest Camino conversations did not take place in Spain but has been here in Australia, with a woman who, although we share the same language and are both veterans of the pilgrim track, has a vastly different background and fore- ground to my own.

The night before Good Friday 2012, a book by Ailsa Piper,

an author quite unknown to me, arrived in the mail. I read it over the Easter weekend. It was about taking on the load of other people's sins. Connections began to form in my mind.

On Friday the parish church is full, listening again to the story of judgement, torture and death. The mood is sober. The message is Jesus 'carrying our sins'—now there's a link! On Sunday, people are lifted with a story of new life and resurrection. This is the normal Easter fare.

But there is a backstory that always catches my attention.

Where were those young friends, apostles we will call them, on the Friday of the execution? They were hiding in a locked room paralysed by fear, staring into the abyss of their own cowardice. All their enthusiastic promises of support were cold ashes in their mouths. The newly risen Christ appears in their locked room. There was no recrimination. No demand for explanation. No mention of broken promises. What he offered them was *shalom*—the ancient blessing of love, under-standing, abundance and fullness of life. What he gave them was forgiveness.

The origins of the Christian story are grounded in the expe-rience of a group of terrified, broken, vulnerable people—not the usual foundation story told of heroes. The Easter event carries a painful reminder that new life often comes in broken-ness. Sometimes in the brokenness of others.

Ailsa's book reminded me that in the far-off Middle Ages, pilgrims attempted a highly unusual way of being connected—by carrying one another's sins. This notion, initially seeming like rank superstition, spoke directly to the Easter story, and seemed to have a surprising foundation of good common sense. I began to ask myself fundamental questions: To what extent are those of us who come together in church a practical community? How are we really connected to one another? How do we take genuine responsibility for each other?

In this monologue world of mine, I talk a great deal about a family of believers supporting one another. We in the Catholic Church claim to be a community whose aim is to take on the task of being a healing agent in the wider world. On a bad day—and those days are becoming more frequent in the light of the stories of abuse—it's hard to recognise such a grand vision.

We build hospitals to help people with broken bodies. We minister to the dying. We teach children. We provide shelter for the homeless and try to share their alienation. We struggle for the rights of refugees. Why, then, do we find it hard to imagine carrying the sins of others? Why do we find it so confronting to face this gospel responsibility?

That's how my conversation with Ailsa began. It wasn't long before the ensuing emails became a vehicle for personal sharing.

We are a generation apart in age—or is that two generations? Ailsa grew up on an immense sheep station in Western Australia. I grew up on Sydney's Lane Cove River. Her life has been in the theatre. My life has been in the Church. She's a walker. I'm more of a swimmer. Our conversation, between Melbourne and Sydney, was by email. Ailsa's language is not always my language. She will use the word 'love' with little restraint. There is a cautious philosopher locked away somewhere in me that wants to make all sorts of distinctions. Ailsa chides me that I'm splitting hairs or just plain fearful. She likes to chide!

Our correspondence grew out of mutual curiosity, and explored many issues—for example, the nature of belief— from two quite disparate points of view. Belief has many faces, it always has had. The battle lines drawn up between believer and unbeliever often seem childish to me, like kids wrestling in a playground. Not that our letters were debates between belief and unbelief at all—but the nature of human belief is never too far away from what occupies our minds.

I like the word 'belief'. It has always intrigued me. The word comes from an old English word *lief*, which can be translated as 'love'. Belief, at its heart, is 'to be in love'. Faith is paying endless loving attention to the meaning of our existence; to be in love with life at its ultimate level.

Perhaps Ailsa is the true believer!

That's not the entire story, of course. Where do we find the time and the vocabulary to tell even part of a person's story? But that will do for a start.

Tony

AUTUMN

Ailsa,

Sandy Gore sent me a copy of your book just before Easter. I simply want to tell you how much I enjoyed it.

Being a parish priest facing Easter celebrations I thought it could wait for a week or two before I got into it—but dammit I made the mistake of reading a couple of pages and it picked me up and wouldn't let me go. Started it on Good Friday and finished red-eyed late Easter Monday morning.

Thanks.

Have read several accounts of pilgrim adventures—none better than yours. I have to confess (nice word in this context) I'm a bit of a Camino junkie—Léon to Santiago 2009; Le Puy-en-Velay to Conques 2010; and a track you might not have heard of, the Cammino delle Dolomiti in Italy 2011.

When I finished the book I had to nail my feet to the floor to stop getting on a plane and heading back. And I hope you realise—it's all your fault.

I caught your conversation with Phillip Adams on ABC radio. Noted that no theologian had responded to the idea of carrying another's sins. It's now my favourite question to ask over dinner—it causes mayhem and wonderful arguments. I'm no professional theologian but I have found the idea a new and fascinating concept about how we are so closely connected and responsible for one another.

If your publisher detects a little spike in the sales figures around the Rose Bay area, I have to shamelessly admit to banging on about it from the pulpit here.

Anyway, just wanted to say thanks and congratulations. You are a gift.

Buen camino.

Tony Doherty

Dear Tony,

I can't tell you how happy it made me to get your letter. I imagine such a book could well have felt like penance when you received it, given the conversations you have in your daily life. I'm very moved that it spoke to you, and even more so that you would spread the word. I will ask my publisher to check for the Rose Bay sales spike—what a glorious area in which to walk and work.

Your letter reminded me of how important it sometimes is for those of us 'in the biz' to reassess our understanding of what we take for granted—whether that be showbiz, writing, walking or caring for the souls of others. I love the idea of you talking sins over dinner—though beware they don't turn into last suppers. I remember the reactions I got when I first mooted the idea. It's a kicker of a word, sin—though I guess you'd know that! I've had reports of some bookstores and libraries not wanting to order the book because it sounded 'salacious'. Hilarious, but it's that word.

And yes, it would be fascinating to hear a professional theologian's perspective. I'm not sure many of them listen to the insightful Mr Adams, given his long-declared atheism.

Don't leave your feet nailed to the floor for too long. You are clearly a natural pilgrim, with a yearning for the road. As we know, it will get you in the end.

Thank you for your generous response, and I sincerely hope we might meet when I'm up in Sydney in June/July. Bell Shakespeare are producing a version of *The Duchess of Malfi*, which I co-adapted some years back. It will be on at the Opera House, and I'm pretty excited about it. Perhaps we could get that Sandy to join us for a wine or a coffee while I'm in town.

For now, though, *buen camino, peregrino . . . y muchas muchas gracias.*

You've made a pilgrim very happy tonight.

Ailsa

Ailsa,

Thanks for the warm reply.

Interesting, your comment about Phillip Adams and his declared atheism. Funnily enough, I see him as a person continually searching into the nature of human belief, perhaps not using classical religious language—but that's one of the reasons he never fails to spark my interest. Classical religious language, not to be abandoned thoughtlessly of course, can sometimes block off genuine enquiry into the mystery which surrounds human belief. Adams, I find, can at times bring real freshness to the conversation.

Would love to meet up with you if that is possible. I will be out of the country—travelling to Africa, in fact—from June 25 to July 25, however.

Happy days.

Tony

Good morning, Tony!

It's the pesky pilgrim. If you can spare it, would you take a minute to consider this?

Today, via Twitter, I was sent a link to an iPhone app. It's called Confession: A Roman Catholic App. It sells for $1.99 and the blurb says that it's 'designed to be used in the confessional' and is 'the perfect aid for every penitent'. It has a personalised examination of conscience for each user, password-protected files and more. There don't seem to be any indulgences or privileges being sold, but as one of my Facebook community asked me: 'Shouldn't the app be free?'

Regardless of cost, it made me wonder again about the sin of 'simony', and my actions. I don't know if you will recall it, but in my book I wrote about receiving an email from one of my 'sinners' when I reached a net café in Córdoba. He asked whether I was guilty of simony, which is, I think, defined as 'the buying or selling of ecclesiastical privileges–for example, pardons'. I was going to take a long walk to consult my conscience, but then I thought– 'Call on Tony!'

So, my theologian to the north, what think you?

Buen camino! (That is my favourite wish and blessing, you know.)

Ailsa

Ailsa,

The plot continues to thicken.

I have been hearing confessions for 50 years. Fewer and fewer people avail themselves of this opportunity. Why? My conviction lies in the belief that moral issues today are more complex and sophisticated than they have ever been in the past. Take for example the whole matter of telling the truth in a rampant PR culture, or the commercial sexualisation of young girls, or how to moderate our lifestyle to avoid the destruction of our environment. How about them for starters?

In the practice of Catholic confession, many people are locked into language and concepts they learned when they were seven years old—and they've never been able to shake free of them. This sort of mind-paralysis renders the conversation trivial, keeping them as obedient children rather than thoughtful adults. When 55-year-old captains of industry come in and talk to me about missing their night prayers, I feel that the Church has trivialised a process which, at its heart and in the right setting, expresses profound belief in the possibility of healing and forgiveness.

But you, Ailsa, with your sin-walking, have stumbled on a vehicle by which people can discharge their distress in a more mature way. You invite your 'sinners' to tell you what weighs them down. You offer to share the weight. And they can't tell you their story quickly enough.

You have nothing to fear from being accused of simony. This is a specific canonical term to describe the selling of sacraments. Your freedom from being able to offer a sacrament (no matter how powerful the confession of friends might in fact be) preserves you from any charge of simony.

The confession app was a bit of a media story here when it broke. What interests me most is that both what you have been doing, and the online story, touch a nerve among many of us to confront the dark sides of our lives in ways which are genuinely liberating. And the real issue you have uncovered is that we can help one another to do that.

Happy days.

Tony

Tony,

Thanks so much.

I'm not sure you are right in saying my 'sinners' couldn't wait to tell their stories. Many I asked were horrified at the notion, or scoffed at the possibility of atonement being possible by my striding across a foreign land. But for those who did volunteer a story, I think it was sometimes painful and cost them dearly. Cost is a big issue for me. I don't think anything worthwhile comes for free, and those who experienced change took risks—not the least being to put their stories into the hands of a fool!

I do have a couple more queries though—was that a groan I heard?—based on a comment you made. You mentioned my 'freedom' from being able to offer a sacrament. Strange choice of words from you, I thought. Do you experience the delivery of sacraments as a burden? And while we're at it, what exactly is a sacrament? I have an understanding from schooldays, but I suspect it may be outdated or naïve. Apologies for replying to an answer with more questions, but your comment did make me sit up.

OK. Enough quizzing. I look forward even more to meeting you. I promise not to bombard you with theological curiosities. Trust Sydney is warmer than down here. We are shivering in our overcoats and mufflers and collecting dried eucalypt branches and gumnuts for our fires. Clear blue skies above, but winter surely approaches.

Ailsa

Ailsa,

What is a sacrament, you ask blithely?

Bit of a stretch to explain in a few words, but here goes. The Christian tradition names a few moments in the human journey—getting married, leaving childhood, coming into a community, confronting our own brokenness, even facing serious illness—as mightily important. But more than that, it names them as deeply human moments. When you have something deeply human—you have 'the sacred'. The sacraments are rituals coming out of the history of the Church designed to say—'let's celebrate their importance'. Let's catch the mystery, catch the sacred. Not allow the significance just to slip away as we, so often, skate over to the rush of the next big distraction.

Sorry, bit of a lecture I know. Let's talk about this more later. It goes to the heart of my understanding of the sacred. Of 'God', if you like.

Is offering these sacraments a burden?

No, I didn't mean that. I'm in the 'sacrament business'. I think it's my best work—marrying people, helping people to face death, celebrating new life. But the Church places sensible boundaries around these key sacred moments, and so I work within those boundaries. That you, Ailsa, can approach other people's troubles, sins if you like, according to your own lights and in your own fashion, is a sort of freedom, I reckon.

If you will indulge me, here's an extract from an article I wrote for an online publication. The piece was sparked by reading your book:

To what extent are we willing to carry the pain of others? In a church which claims to be a supporting community of believers—how do we give hope, in some genuine fashion, to someone whose life is fast unravelling?

For Catholics, facing with horror the shocking events of child abuse and sexual manipulation, how do we stop from drowning ourselves? One familiar response is denial. 'It can't be happening.' 'Just a few rotten apples.' Another response is angrily scapegoating whatever easy target comes to mind, or rather shamefully pulling the blankets over our heads and pretending it will go away.

Are we strong enough to carry the pain of others—say, the victims of this terrible abuse. Or an even more unspeakable possibility—to carry a little of the disgrace of those seen as responsible.

Hate to tell you but it is T-shirt weather up here in my home town.

Happy days.

Tony

Dear Tony,

You write about confronting brokenness, and it makes me wonder what it might look like for the church communities to carry the disgrace of abusers. Or of those who enabled them. To carry sin for them might be too much for these shoulders, I think. I try to remember that the label 'monster' is too quick, too simplistic, but I picture the children and my heart's reflex is to harden.

Thank you for opening up my understanding of sacraments. I wish someone had made that simple conjunction–sacred moment–years ago. It may not be the exact etymology, but it affords me a way to approach the idea in the religious sense, and also in my own life. Those sacred human moments to which you alluded are not to be glossed over or lost in the rush, I agree. Rather like the way nature asks us to observe the changing seasons, perhaps? Those moments mark transitions in our lives, and they should be honoured.

Do you know the American poet, Mary Oliver? She is one of my prophets. I think she would resonate with the word 'sacrament'. I suspect many poets would. They are observers of sacredness. I turn to them when

I need wisdom, comfort or expansion. In Mary's case, I also get my eyes opened afresh to the natural world, my 'heaven'.

T-shirt weather up there? What a sybaritic sort of city Sydney is.

Gracias yet again!

Ailsa

Careful! Some of my best friends are sybarites.

Thanks for the warm reply. Glad you like the article.

You're right onto it about poets. Recently I stumbled on Seamus Heaney talking about his 'sacramental imagination'. Poets, I believe, see below the surface of things to their sacred depths. Those depths are exactly what Christian sacraments alert us to.

Your comment about the difficulty of carrying the disgrace of an abuser is not hard for me to understand. But I want to stretch people's imagination to what carrying the sins of others might mean. Sometimes it's not too pretty.

I have never been too comfortable at hasty judgements—even about the most horrendous events. Any comment I might make about the perpetrators screams out that I am being defensive and totally insensitive because I am a priest myself. Can't deny that possibility—nor do I want to. But let me ask you to entertain for a moment the possibility of someone in prison for child sexual abuse writing to you for help—from the hellish well of his despair. What does one say?

Carrying another person's sin—better use the word crime for what we are talking about—comes in many forms and at many levels.

Happy days.

Tony

Hi Tony,

No, 'pretty' it surely isn't, the carrying of sins. I felt grief often as I struggled with the weight I hefted along the road, meditating on what people had told me. I want very much to believe of myself that I can see the humanity, or the potential humanity, in anyone; that I can locate compassion in myself for some aspect of their story. But the abuse stories trigger something bloody in me. I think I could possibly stretch to murderers and rapists with more ease than those who injure children, be they parents, siblings, strangers—or priests. My best intentions scatter like leaves. But then you ask me—what if someone reaches out to you? Would I have you tell them they are beyond help?

No. No I wouldn't. I recognise the abusers are unwell, no matter how much I might want to cast them as evil or villains.

I can see no such illness in those who covered up the abuse, though. That crime is too ghastly. But I guess the real question you pose is whether or not I could stretch myself to carry those sins if I were asked. All I can say is that one thing I learned on my long road in Spain is that it would be unwise for me to second-guess my abilities. They are both bigger and smaller than I imagine. We know very little of our capacities till they are tested.

I'm grateful for the questions you pose and your observations, even if they do give me pause.

On a trivial note, I googled you and loved that I could see a picture of you, grinning broadly. Now I will know who to spot across a crowded café. Isn't it strange that we're able to find out so much about each other on the internet, and so quickly? If we had been writing to each other twenty years ago, I would have had to send you a description of my physical appearance and of my working life. So much of that is out there in the clouds, now, just waiting for us to press 'search'. We search and search, and I guess sometimes we do find a bit of meaning, or at least connection. But I wonder if something hasn't been lost. I still love my handwritten snail mail.

Oh I'm a Luddite. The world's most connected Luddite, a friend once called me. It's kind of true, but I have to confess to being very chuffed when I saw your smiling face on my computer screen just now.

Buen camino!

Ailsa

Ailsa,

Hasty note.

Checked your Sydney schedule on your blog—smart, aren't I? Didn't even have to go to your Facebook profile. Your book left me with many indelible impressions of you. Try not to disappoint, will you?

Any chance of having a quick bite to eat on the 21st after your book signing? If you have other plans there might be some time on the 20th or earlier, about lunchtime, on the 21st.

Be careful. Never trust a publicity shot.

Tony

Hi Tony,

'Publicity shot.' The two most terrifying words I know. One of the reasons I stopped acting. Agh!

The evening of the 21st is already booked, but the days of the 20th and 21st are both free. I will be staying in Lewisham, close to the train, so can get to pretty much anywhere. And I would love it!

Let me know what would suit you best, and I will be there. And wear a carnation in your buttonhole, please. Just for the old-fashioned fun of it.

Ailsa

Ailsa,

If the 20th is still free, how about lunch, say about 12.30. I'll be at our parish school's sports carnival. If this works I will find a place around Lewisham and we can work out the details.

Happy days.

Tony

Hi Tony,

I will put it in the diary this minute. Details later, but we are locked in. *Gracias!*

I'm off to splash through some puddles. It's raining again.

Ailsa

Ailsa,

Had dinner with Sandy last night. If you are still free on June 21 (we had a plan for June 20), she could join us. Are you?

Happy days.

Tony

Dear Tony,

Yes, freeeeeeeeeeeeeee on June 21, and Sandy's presence will be a gift. Just fancy. Two actresses and a Monsignor. I fear there is a joke lurking there, though I'm not an actress anymore, and quite glad of it.

Still, I can't resist telling you a quick story from back in the dim dark past when I was still performing. As a young thing, I played Bubba, the little neighbour in Ray Lawler's classic Oz play, *Summer of the Seventeenth Doll*. The newspaper review came out, and the final line was clearly meant to read '. . . and Ailsa Piper is good as Bubba.'

The sub-editor obviously had a field day with that lukewarm praise and it came out in the paper reading

'. . . and ALISSA PIPPER is GOD as BUDDA.' The sub-editor may have got my name wrong, but I'd like you to remember who you are talking to when we meet!

Looking forward so much.

Ailsa

Ailsa,

Do I look for a short, tubby, bare-bellied figure with a smile? And did you write the sub-editor a stiff letter?

The meal on Thursday is at 12.30. I have arranged it near the Opera House as Sandy is working there. East Chinese Restaurant is the name.

It's not your Spanish *menú del día*. Hope Chinese is OK.

Happy days.

Tony

Thanks very much, Tony.

That sounds brilliant. Chinese is wonderful. I will be there with a big anticipatory grin–so excited to be meeting you, and seeing Sandy. Thanks for organising us.

Buen camino, pilgrim.

Ailsa (God-as-Buddha) Piper

DEAR READER,

Time moves in one direction, memory in another. Lots of us mistake our imagination for our memory. I know I do, and the tendency becomes more frequent as the years unfold.

Throwing my mind back to the first meeting with this writer whose work had so intrigued me, I recall one of those sunny winter's days in June—the best Sydney has to offer. So, where does one entertain a visitor from the elegant city of Melbourne? Find a place close to the harbour, buzzy with ferries, in the shadow of the Opera House. That should do it. They talk about 'power dressing'—this might be called 'power entertaining'.

To be perfectly honest, I approached the chosen Chinese restaurant with a wee touch of apprehension. Confronted with an aged cleric who had introduced himself to her by a series of emails, would this young pilgrim be flexible enough to deal with the cold reality of white hair and wrinkles?

My anxiety dissolved before we finished our salt and pepper prawns. The conversation was lively, the food delicious, and a glass of Tasmanian Riesling kept the boat nicely afloat. With the other guests, a prodigiously gifted actress and a Catholic nun of keen intelligence, the conversation was both zippy and spirited. Anecdotes about the theatre, the day's political news (asylum seekers were in the headlines again), that always pleasing discovery of identifying mutual friends, even arcane subjects of theology were explored. I found myself occupying the role of listener. This, I must quickly admit, might not be the recollection of others. Memory and imagination, as I have already observed, are slippery critters.

One of the oddest connections unfolded when I told Ailsa that I'd been unable to sleep in the early hours of that same day, and had listened to a fascinating story on radio about a gritty New Zealand psychologist running a program of rehabilitation among the most hardened prisoners in his country. My distinct feeling had been that I must have been the only person in this country listening to radio about such an odd topic at such an unfashionable hour. To my utter astonishment, Ailsa had been listening to the same program at the same ungodly time—and she had shared my excitement about what we'd heard. An amazing connection.

What are my other enduring memories of meeting this new email friend of a short three months? Instantly engaging, vivacious, hardworking, and intensely committed to the task, whether it was walking, acting, directing, or writing across several quite different genres—such as adapting the text of a 17th-century play, crafting a radio script, or recounting her pilgrimage of carrying the sins of others across Spain. All of this while maintaining rich and frequent contact with an unimaginably vast network of friends living in every corner of the world. I felt I was swimming in waters just a little out of my depth. Ailsa's enthusiasm and joie de vivre were apparent in both her book and the letters we had exchanged, and they shone out in her welcome. To that date my only image of Ailsa had been a blurred and rather sketchy photograph on the inside flyleaf of her celebrated Camino memoir. The publisher should be sued. The reality was so different—in focus, she was bright of eye and wide of smile.

Another twist in this long lunch turned to Ireland and the magic of storytelling. After nourishment, shelter and companionship, the Irish believe stories are the thing we need most in the world. Our individual recollections of that meeting might not perfectly match, but one thing we both remember was a story I told. Don't know when I first heard it or even where it came from. All I know is that it had been floating around my memory bank waiting to find a mooring. Allow me to expand the story here, as I did that afternoon.

In some far-off age, within every Irish village, the three most highly regarded figures in town were the priest, the policeman and the keeper of the story. (I'm not even sure that was the precedence, but I'm the one telling and I'm sticking to that order of things.) The storyteller enjoyed the colourful Irish name of 'the shanachie'. As I vigorously interrogated my lunch companion about the stories she had written or performed—had to beat it out of her, if the truth be told—my memory began to stir about the organisation of this Irish village. Here I was in the presence of a living, breathing modern day shanachie. She spoilt it, of course, by having the unmistakably Scottish name of Ailsa and genes that go back to the rocky west coast of that 'land o' the leal',

40

but sticking to details never has nor ever will distract me from a good tale.

So here we all were sitting over the San Choy Bau. We had the shanachie and the priest, but alas neither of our two other charming guests could be vaguely mistaken for a police officer. Perhaps one of them may have had some odd member of the constabulary tucked away in the family tree but they kept mum about it.

Although I must admit that I lack watertight evidence for the veracity of this Irish legend, I can claim to have once met and been entertained by a genuine and contemporary shanachie. The place was in the wild north-west of Ireland, in the little Donegal village of Derryveagh. It was the birth-place of my father's father, whose family had been forcibly ejected from their tiny cottage by a rapacious landlord named John Adair, who in April 1861 evicted 250 tenants from his property.

I had travelled there with an Australian film crew that was visiting the village to research and record the history of this now quite famous eviction. Half a dozen villagers directed us to the keeper of the 140-year-old story, who turned out to be an ancient Donegal widow—probably 90-something—with the name of Kitty Duddy. 'Kitty will sing you the story. Her own mother did and her mother before her.'

I sat at Kitty's kitchen table in front of a fuel stove and a heating kettle, and she sang the story of 'The Ballad of Cruel John Adair' as the camera rolled. Kitty had no pretension about her voice, she had no sense of stage or lighting, she just sat on the kitchen chair and sang. For me it was mesmerising. It was the sacred scripture of my family's life, and from then on the indispensable role of the storyteller was etched in my mind.

Stories, indeed, are life itself. They bring together the elegant dance of memory and imagination in all of us. Of all the fun and frivolity of that first meal with Ailsa, and the connections that surfaced between us, it was the power of story and the sheer joy of shared tales that linger with me. That was the fuel that motivated our continuing exchange of letters. It still does.

Happy days.

Tony

DEAR READER,

I just went to my computer's image folder to find a particular photo from the day I met Tony. In the shot, I'm wearing Melbourne black from head to toe, a pair of red patent boots, and a crimson scarf is slung around my shoulders. We are under the colonnade of the walk to the Opera House. I'm in profile, laughing at something Tony has said, my hair out of control in the wind. He's wearing a navy jacket and a grin. He looks rather like a cheery pirate.

I couldn't find the image. I searched and searched to no avail. Then I realised—it doesn't exist. There is no such photo! And yet, I recall that picture as clear as day. It's etched in my memory; we're held in time, framed.

Memory and imagination are, as Tony says, slippery little suckers. It's easy to convince yourself that something is fact when it has been viewed by the mind's eye. That particular retina loves to embellish and gild. I remember all the things he describes, but my imagined snapshot distils them into smiles, primary colours and laughter. Breezy and bright. That was the tone of the day.

Tony might also claim that my propensity to exaggerate was what made me tell him, when we met, that I felt I already knew him. He still finds that a bit wacky, but my sense of deep knowing wasn't made up, and my memory of it is entirely accurate. When I first saw him, I remember thinking, 'Ah! There you are.' It was as though I had been waiting a very long time.

I've felt this before. Once, out on a Camino road in Spain with a fellow pilgrim. Effortless connection. Instant trust and knowing. I've also felt it with one or two of my intimate friends. I have vivid recall of those meetings as a kind of homecoming, long before we'd uttered ten words.

Funnily enough, I didn't feel that when I met my husband, Peter. That encounter was all newness and discovery, curiosity and fascination–even though I'd seen and admired him as an actor. Although we fell toward each other in a rush, and decided to get married within weeks of meeting, in some ways, mystery still categorises Peter for me. It may seem curious to say that after more than 27 years of shared life, but perhaps it's why we came together: to learn about, and from, each other. I believe relationships are our greatest teachers, and the more they evolve–via attending or arguing, sharing or diverging–the more we expand as human beings. And that's one of our main jobs in life, I reckon–to help one another to grow.

I couldn't have known at any of the meetings I've described how vital those people would become to me, or how much I would change as a result of knowing them. I simply had to leave myself open to my instincts, and trust. Which is the thing I felt with Tony. Trust. Not because he was a priest–that was more likely to induce expectations of piety or remoteness–but because he listened without judgement and, as time progressed, he did the hard yards. So, regardless of the instant relief and recognition that is my abiding memory of our first face-to-face meeting, he didn't rest on laurels. He worked at the friendship. He still does.

There are two other things I recall from that day. Firstly, he didn't 'fess up to it being his birthday until he insisted on paying for our lunch, and secondly, he seemed to know half of Sydney! Every group coming through the door of the restaurant greeted him. Or am I making that up?

Memory . . .

It's hard for a storyteller to be completely honest when dealing with memory. The thing is, dear Reader, I want you to feel the possibility I felt at that meeting–to sense the whirl of the conversation, the spice of the food and the amazement at the rapport. I want you to understand how pleasing it was that the real person was exactly the person I'd met in our letters. I want you to be there with me, captivated by the sparkling water outside and the sparkling words inside.

The others at the table were equally compelling, I should say. Sandy's connection to Tony was another coincidence that amazed us. She is a brilliant actor and a woman of gravitas, humour and heart. I am indebted to Peter for her presence in my days. They were actors together in their twenties, and the stories of those times, touring rural Australia on trucks and in buses, always make me rock with laughter. Sandy met Tony when he was an adviser on a TV series called *Brides of Christ* decades ago, and they remained friends. Patty Fawkner, who was the other guest, is a great friend of Tony's and a woman of penetrating insight. She challenged my school-girl notions of what the word 'nun' meant. About my age, and possessed of a razor-sharp mind, she made me laugh and left me curious.

One of the things I remember best, though, was Tony's tale of the shanachie, the priest and the copper in the Irish village. It enchanted me. Now, when I think of those three people, they don't live in some boggy village in Donegal. They inhabit a world of glistening water, Chinese food and ferries. They live at Circular Quay.

Sydney is the place I chose when I left Perth, back in 1982. It's where I was living when I met Peter, in 1986. He proposed to me by the harbour in Rushcutters Bay. Sydney is also the home of some of my oldest friends, so regular visits north were part of my life in Melbourne from the time I moved there, in 1987.

Places have layers. They are overwritten with our stories. The harbour holds many of mine, though I will never have as many watery stories as Tony. His memories of Sydney Harbour are endless–and often on repeat! I enjoy them all, though I suspect some of them are more the work of imagination than memory. No matter. They always gladden me, like the shimmer of sun on salt water, or the first drops of rain on parched red earth.

Ailsa

WINTER

Dear Tony,

So, your birthday is done for the year.

What a sly dog you are! Why didn't you mention we were meeting on such an auspicious day? I feel so lucky to have celebrated with you–but remember, there has to be another lunch so I can treat you next time. You did promise.

Thank you for the warmth of the welcome into your life; for the conversation, which feels like it could extend so far; for the breadth and depth of your knowledge, shared so easily; for the twinkle in your eye and the spring you put in my step.

I hope your trip to Africa is uplifting and restorative–it sounds such an adventure.

I will think of your big brother and walk with him in my heart. I hope his health will improve. Would love to hear more of your childhood together. It sounds idyllic to this desert-born woman.

I send great swathes of gratitude, and the hope that we can continue this conversation for a long, long time. Thanks for such a happy, celebratory first meeting. Or was it a first meeting? I do feel I've known you forever.

Travel very safe.

Ailsa

Ailsa,

It was good, wasn't it?

Not so much a surprise for me. You have shared a little of the dimension of your mind and your heart in writing—so generously. So I was prepared for what turned out to be a delicious meeting, even though I was somewhat under the weather.

The most intriguing moment, as I think back on the lunch, was Nigel Latta and his book *Into the Darklands and Beyond*. I couldn't believe anyone on Planet Earth would share my enthusiasm for what he had to say—a man who went into prisons to deal with serious sexual abusers, and set himself parameters regarding those who he believed could be rehabilitated and those who, he said (in the bluntest of language), could not. I cannot remember ever listening to the *Law Report* before—5.30 am no less. And then I struggled out of bed to scribble his name down.

So to have you recognise what I was talking about and to have remembered him was eerie. I don't know where you fit that into your philosophy of coincidence, O Horatio, but for me—I come from a long line of Celtic witches who understand such things.

Talking to you about my brother and how tough he is doing it at the moment, and of the Lane Cove River, had me recall a memory which goes right back to the age of five. Dostoyevsky wrote—'One good memory may be the means of saving us.' Let me tell you one of mine, since you asked.

Something I've not told you is that I swim in the harbour every morning. If the truth be told, I'm more of a swimmer than a walker. It was over 75 years ago—you weren't even a glint in your mother's eye back then, sunshine!—that I learned to swim. This is how it happened . . .

Sunday mornings in January were so hot that you could almost hear the gum tips crackle in the sun. My father, my skinny older brother and I would trek through the bush with my little rubber swimming ring, picking our way carefully in single file along a scarcely identifiable track, alert for the rustle of a snake, or perhaps a blue-tongue, even the occasional goanna. Our destination: the baths at Tambourine Bay. I struggled to keep up. In this dense bush, you never knew what critter would attack you.

On the track, there was dark mystery. Half-overgrown with lantana and tick bush was a square hewn out of sandstone, filled with fetid, slime-covered water known as 'the convict pool'. Why was it there, what purpose would it have served, who were the convicts who shaped it? All unanswered questions to feed a five-year-old's imagination.

After the lurking dangers of the bush, and struggling over slippery rocks, the sight of the baths was sheer relief. The rickety wooden structure had solid planked decks at both ends, a springy diving board, and wooden ladders to help swimmers back to the safety of the deck. Sun-splashed water lapped just below the deck.

My brother and I raced each other to get out of our clothes and into the water. But the contest was grossly unfair. I couldn't swim. Dad had to inflate the rubber ring for me, then secure it carefully with a stopper. Infuriating delay, every time. The skinny one always beat me to the water.

There is a moment in life—never to be dismissed lightly—when we have to leave the ring behind.

One day, I jumped.

I took a deep breath and let go—thrashing around in the water, flailing arms and legs inventing some sort of primitive dog paddle, mouth full of Lane Cove River, and a desperate feeling of sinking to the bottom, lost forever.

A skinny arm reached out and grabbed me.

A never-to-be-forgotten moment.

My brother gave me my confidence in the water. My freedom. Every day when I dive into the harbour, he is with me.

Thanks for taking me back to that summer. Dostoyevsky was right.

Blessings on Sandy for introducing me to such a rich, searching and thoroughly delightful pilgrim. Or have I here another Celtic witch?

Tony

Dear Tony,

Now I'm crying. I feel life is a continuous attempt to let go of rings, don't you?

It's a lovely tribute to that skinny older brother, now carried on your emotional shoulders—or so it seems to me.

I note your confession that you are more of a swimmer than a walker. My confession is that I actually can't swim! Well, I manage a kind of timid breaststroke, a gasping dog paddle and a flat-on-my-back kickalong. Pathetic, I know. But I did grow up in red dirt, you'll recall. Water was a novelty in the Gascoyne. One of my few actual childhood memories is of tottering down to the creekbed with my ever-patient paternal grandfather. We would sit in the sand and dig down with our hands until the hole began to fill with sweet-smelling water. It's such a particular scent, water rising through river sand. Wish I could dab it behind my ears, that smell of stillness and possibility.

Anyway, your story made me ponder how we are formed in childhood, and I offer this anecdote by way of a pointer to my infatuation with walking.

My maternal grandmother, known as Ning, was a mixture of misty Irish softness from her parents and Aussie bush resilience from her surroundings. She was also something of a tracker. Out on the red earth she could decipher meanings in a squiggle, the message in a cracked twig. As an illustration of this, my mother, writing an account of my life for me just before she died, told of one occasion when, as a three-year-old, I escaped the watchful eyes of all my minders and set off on a grand safari with Mitzi the fox-terrier.

Noticing my absence, a panic-stricken group began to search, but it was Ning who picked up the tracks of the adventurers and caught up with us. Mitzi was in front, while I followed, collecting Everlasting daisies.

My mother reported that the hapless Mitzi got a serious whacking and was left to follow the jeep home, while I was fussed over in the front seat, and checked from top to toe for bites, stings or structural damage. Cossetted. Adored.

My inheritance from Ning and Mum was the confidence to walk the world expecting only flowers and wonder, safe in the knowledge that even if lost, I will always be found. I hadn't considered it till your story, so thank you, *compañero*.

Gracias. In Spanish, it means 'grace', you know.

Ailsa

Ailsa,

Now here is a connection you might not have been expecting . . .

The Gospels tell us that Jesus walked everywhere.

There is a reason for this.

When one walks one can also talk, one can stop and have time for others, one can eat and touch people and interact with them. Walking allows us a particular life-pace. It makes possible a way of understanding and looking with open eyes;

it is about having a capacity to make visible what is invisible; of paying attention to inconvenient suffering; of taking responsibility for what is broken in our world whether it is wounded people or a damaged environment.

You know this, of course.

But I wonder if you ever consider that other walker as you step out into the world.

Tony

Dear Tony,

Don't wish to sound grand, but I have been told often of a tradition of walking mysticism. Holy men and women who take to the road. Prophets, saints and other teachers. Hadn't considered it before, but Jesus is often 'on the road' isn't he? Maybe that is why I think of the road as a sacred place.

You are spot on with your reflections about the pace of walking and what it brings. Why didn't bible studies tell me that when I was little? Clearly you had better teachers.

Now, I have a favour to ask. Throw a few more memories my way, would you? I loved that picture of the little boy amid the blue-tongues. I'd like more. Maybe a potted history? Even your CV? Anything that comes to mind. Our backgrounds were so different—me in the bush, and you in your big watery city of Sydney. How about it? I mean, what else do you have to do other than entertain your new pen-pal?

Buen camino from the wandering tyke with her arms full of Everlastings.

Ailsa

Ailsa,

'Three feet of ice are not frozen in one day,' the Chinese say. Nor are eight decades easily summarised in a few lines. But one word from the Captain, and I drop my preparation for the three weddings this weekend, and spring to attention. Here goes ... hang on to your hat.

Let me begin with a few scattered memories: our Lane Cove family home being threatened by the '38 bushfires;

being taken to the school's basement air raid shelter when the midget subs attacked Sydney; seeing Frank 'the dancing man' McAlary waltzing down Martin Place at war's end; rattling across the Harbour Bridge in a toast-rack tram with the conductor hanging perilously on the outside (how I dreamed of being a risk-taking conductor one day); riding the waves at Curl Curl for hours on a rubber surf-o-plane; bringing a school mate to my home and being asked 'Are you rich or poor?' and having no idea what he meant; being dressed up by Mum as Mae West, complete with cigarette holder, at the Sans Souci guest house at Katoomba when I was five, or was it four; trips to Manly with Mum so I could cure my whooping cough by inhaling the sea air—it was a bloody long way, and we had to take three buses to get there; Sunday tucker—kidneys on toast, boiled eggs and shallots, cold rice and milk, roast lamb, mashed potato and peas; drinking Coca-Cola for the first time—brought by American sailors to Sydney; chewing gum in long strips rather than the little white pillows; attending my first live show—*The Gondoliers!*—at the glamorous-beyond-belief Theatre Royal; eating Balmoral pudding on summer holidays at a guest house in Terrigal; trying to stay still during the sermon of the impossibly old, white-haired

Monsignor on a steamy Sunday morning; seeing the first screening of *Gone With the Wind* with Mum and her friends when I was four or five—Mum couldn't believe her little wriggler stayed still and quiet for the whole four hours.

Today, for some reason or other, I feel far more sympathy for white-haired Monsignors searching for Sunday morning words.

Strange, isn't it? No matter how busy I am, there's something deeply satisfying about fishing events from childhood out of my memory. It's a wet Sunday afternoon habit of mine. But these intimate disclosures don't come for free, you know. What's your memory like, my young friend? How about applying yourself to the same task?

I'm off to turn on the lights and attend to the brides.

Tony

Dear Tony,

Thank you, my white-haired Monsignor. Actually, I feel a tinge of sympathy for you today. Three weddings!

How you must marvel at Sydney when you zoom around in your silver hatchback. The layers of history—trams rattling (I must find out when they stopped); midget subs (ever feel nervous when you're swimming?); air raid shelters and American sailors bearing gifts. Such palimpsest in those streets of yours, layers painted over and over with stories and changes.

Must admit, I'd like to have seen you togged up as Mae West. Was this some particular form of maternal torture? And your complete innocence about whether you were rich or poor really struck me. If only we could hang onto that ignorance. So much time is wasted worrying about how much we do or don't have, when we, in Australia, mostly have plenty of everything. Perhaps our real poverty is in our unwillingness to acknowledge that we could make do with less and share more.

Good grief. Now I'm sounding like a preacher.

I envy you your memories. Such images don't come easily to me, no matter how I dive for them. I've always comforted myself with a line attributed to Ingrid Bergman—'Happiness is good health and a bad memory.' That's me, Monsignor. Were I to spend a rainy Sunday afternoon looking over my shoulder, there would be very few memories before the age of about seventeen. Fragments only. Mostly I rely on photos and anecdotes, but I do recall the smell of the waterbag on a hot still afternoon, and I can remember being shocked at the noise made by the ocean when I first saw it. No one had told me it roared. There are sensory snippets–the taste of home-made cumquat jam smeared on Mum's drop scones; the crinkly texture of those pink Everlastings; the smell of Brylcreem when I hugged my grandfather; the click-clack of the heavy wooden rosary beads that hung from Sister Michael's waist; the muffled sound of Dad's voice behind the office door as he talked on the pedal wireless. I do remember when we first got a TV, after we had moved south, and Mum stuck a layer of purple cellophane over the screen. It was supposed to make the picture clearer, I think. Can't imagine why.

Isn't it odd? Just listing off those little memories was quite easy. Maybe telling myself I couldn't remember took the heat off. Or perhaps I should just stop saying I can't remember. Maybe my brain has started to believe its own publicity. Regardless, I don't feel quite so inadequate.

Thanks, Antonio. A gift, you gave me.

Who was the dancing man you mentioned, please? And what on earth is Balmoral pudding? We had Golden Syrup dumplings, but I've never heard of that. Is it a west coast/east coast thing? A city/country thing? Or heaven forfend, generational?

Tell those brides to wait. I need some answers.

Ailsa

Ailsa,

You don't know Balmoral pudding? What sort of deprived childhood did you have? Picture a large light-coloured mound of pudding topped with custard dribbling down its sides. Sort of spotted dick without the spots.

On the day peace was declared in 1945 'an anonymous dancing man' was photographed in Sydney's Martin Place. The photograph became a famous moment of exuberance felt by all. Frank McAlary was the dancer—a friend of mine who at the time was a cash-strapped law student, who, when all was said and done, really wasn't much of a dancer.

I feel enormously lucky to be able to remember so much.

Tony

Hello lucky man!

This is the deprived child from the south. Hope the brides were all on time, and that Balmoral pud was served at the receptions.

You must be getting so excited about your trip. I'm not envious. Not a bit. No, really. I'm not.

Actually, I write because I was just sent a quote from Paul Theroux remarking on the difference between tourists (lightly disparaging of them) and travellers. It reminded me of the phrase given to me by a hotel clerk in Córdoba: 'A tourist makes demands for many things, whereas a pilgrim gives thanks even when given nothing.' You are a pilgrim, so I know you will travel with a light and grateful heart.

I'm writing a little travel piece at the moment–a pilgrimage of bookshops. I'm so moved by the way they create community. They are 'holy places' for me, because their owners are the custodians of our stories. A sacred responsibility.

Thank you again for the CD you gave me at lunch. The music is so evocative of the mysterious nature of the whole pilgrim undertaking. I played it last night, after watching a documentary on Woody Allen. Strange pairing but it worked! Have I mentioned my love of *Annie Hall*, by the way? Do you know it?

Happy preparations. I will look forward to your return, and to our next meeting.

Buen camino! My favourite blessing on a favourite pilgrim.

Ailsa

Ailsa,

You have to stop doing that!

Talking about Paul Theroux, I mean. Believe it or not I'm currently reading *Fresh Air Fiend: Travel Writings*. At least he didn't quote the snippet you mentioned. Not yet anyway. Haven't finished.

I know reading two books at a time is the sign of an under-developed and restless mind. I have to admit (excuse me, confess is the word) to reading three and sometimes four at once. Beyond help. I need some yet-to-be-invented twelve-step program to assist my rehabilitation.

And while we are at it—another coincidence—Woody! You may be talking to the only Monsignor in Christendom who owns the written scripts of four of his films (including *Annie Hall* herself).

You know, after reading your book, I have become a bit more conscious of what I pack. Did you really weigh your shoelaces? Good Lord, woman. Obsessive doesn't even begin to describe you.

Me, I am very haphazard about socks and phone chargers, but I never leave Australia without lifting a glass to James and Mary Doherty and their two-year-old John. They're my Donegal great-grandparents who, having been evicted from their home in the tiny village of Derryveagh, climbed aboard *The Abyssinian* with their few possessions to make a twenty-week voyage south through the Atlantic and across the freezing Southern Ocean, to hit the coast of Oz somewhere about Victoria's Great Ocean Road. As I watch my in-flight movie I try to get my head around an almost unimaginable voyage like that with a two-year-old. Imposs- ible to picture it.

The story of any family, any people, is carried in its scars. Well, the story of the Derryveagh evictions is a tale of an uprooted people, travelling down a road devoid of hope, heading to an unknown future. Never knew about it in my childhood. Don't even think Mum and Dad knew. This is it in a nutshell:

James was thirty, Mary twenty-eight. They had one child, little John, and she was pregnant with another. They were tenants on a property in the wild hills of Ireland's Donegal. The property owner had plans to import black- faced sheep and wanted to clear the tenants off his land, so a charge of collusion to murder was brought against them—250 men, women and children. The 'crowbar men' accompanied by the local police knocked the roofs of their houses down and evicted them lock, stock and barrel into a bitter northern Irish winter. A grim example of the flakey justice of the time.

With remarkable luck, I discovered the man who supported the voyage of so many refugees of those days. There were thousands of them. His name was John McEncroe, an Irish priest regarded as a hero by Sydney's Catholic community. He set up the Donegal Relief Fund, enabling James and Mary to escape the Letterkenny workhouse (where they would surely have died), and travel to Australia.

And, my shanachie friend, how's this for coincidence? More than a century later, I was appointed Dean of Sydney's St Mary's Cathedral, only to discover that McEncroe's grave lies in its crypt. An astonishing cycle of history.

And now here I am, about to retrace some of their steps in the air-conditioned comfort of a Boeing 747. To repeat the old line—life is not entirely fair. Certainly not for those whose lives are in the hands of someone with a lust for power or property, and little or no conscience.

Which reminds me—I must book to see your *Duchess of Malfi* when I return. A bit of lust and power-play there, isn't there?

You know, I'm scarcely thinking about 'away' at the moment—having too much fun here talking to you. So stop distracting me please—I have to concentrate on some packing.

Happy days.

Tony

Spooky! Witchy, even! Your email arrived just as I was typing your name.

I loved your reflections, but the tale of your ancestors sent a chill through me. It's exactly the story of the refugees we're seeing now, arriving in their frail boats. We need more McEncroes.

And yes, incredible coincidence that you should have been working where he lies–I'd like to have seen your face when you discovered that connection.

Peter and I travelled to Ireland a few years back. We both have some Guinness in our blood–him more than me. That little island has been worked over and over by such cruel forces, yet there's so much life and laughter there. Darkness, too. Signs of the black dog of depression everywhere. But for song and malarkey and poetry–where else would you go?

I particularly recall one evening, walking home through silent dark lanes in Sligo, on the north-west coast. Yeats country. A pilgrimage of sorts for me, to the home of a favourite poet . . .

'But one man loved the pilgrim soul in you . . .'

I've returned to that poem for decades. I think I know it, then I find something else in it.

All Sligo seemed to be sleeping that night, the little one-up-one-down houses shuttered and dark. Peter and I rounded a corner and there was a slant of yellow light falling onto the cobbles, and a rhythmic murmur wafted to us on the night air. We reached the opening–one of those wooden doors, like a stable, with an upper and lower half–and leaned our heads in. It was a tiny room, perhaps originally a parlour. There were four people sitting against the walls on benches, and a miniscule makeshift counter in the far corner where whiskey bottles stood in a neat row. The man behind the counter beckoned us in, motioning us to be silent so as not to disturb the ancient 'leprechaun' who was reciting an epic poem in Gaelic.

The sounds were all swish and softness, but the waves of emotion were clear–excitement, sorrow, hope, grief. The audience of three listened with rapt attention, nodding occasional agreement or wiping a tear, barely registering us as we sipped our whiskey and held our breath. It was mesmerising. The old man was a shanachie, I suppose! I have no idea what was being said, but I got every bit of the story. It was a tale of loss and valour, and of the inheritance of grief. It was a tale of survivors; people like your James and Mary, perhaps.

Then there was applause and hugs for all, including the kangaroo interlopers, and a song or two and more whiskey, and we were required to tell a little of our stories, and when finally we wandered back into the street at 3 am, we were glowing. We were family.

The old man called me *macushla* when he hugged me. I don't know the meaning of it–maybe you do?–but it struck a chord because my grandmother, Ning, used to call me Macushla Macree. I don't know if I've spelled it properly, but I loved to hear her say it, and I loved to hear it on that old man's lips with his thick accent.

Oh, I'm getting all sentimental now. Enough! Really. Pack your rucksack and don't weigh your shoelaces!

Ailsa

Ailsa,

You may never realise how easily Irish stories can divert me. Your image of the rough bar—just great. I could sniff the whiskey on the breath of the old man.

One of the sunny memories of primary school was the practice of our teachers, when the pressures of exams were over, to have us sit back while they read us stories. Warm happy memories. Our young minds didn't have to strain over some half-understood mathematical puzzle or a boring grammatical construction—just relax and be caught up in the magic of storytelling. It was all joy. I wonder sometimes whether even the teachers appreciated how important those sessions were. I'll never forget how I felt listening to them.

You're a real shanachie, you know. I suppose that's what creating theatre and the craft of the writer is all about.

I think I might have come to the appreciation of storytelling a bit later than you, but there is a healthy dose of it in my game, too. The best tradition of the Gospels, indeed all of the bible, is carried in story form. If we're worth our salt at all, we priests should be compelling storytellers.

The Irish had a keen appreciation of this. They saw the shanachie as a physician for damaged memory. Without our stories, they were convinced, we perish.

Now, you asked about the old Irish word *macushla*. Well I do know it. It's a Gaelic word meaning 'my darling'. You're not old enough, of course, but it was the title of a song that goes back to the 1930s or 40s. Have strong memories of my ambitious mother at the piano coaxing me to sing it in my shaky boy soprano. She also harboured plans for me to be an accomplished pianist. Hated practising. At about the age of nine I fell out of a tall tree at a school I was attending— Riverview College—and smashed up my arm. All I could think was—thank God, no more boring piano scales.

But my mother had other ideas.

While I was relishing being free from piano practice, the doctors in the hospital emergency ward were examining a seriously crushed nerve in my elbow. With a certain trepidation,

I am sure, they informed my distraught mother—'Mrs Doherty, your son has suffered a shocking injury. It looks like the only two possibilities are that he will have a withered arm for the rest of his life, or we will have to amputate.'

'Yes, go ahead and amputate by all means,' my mother said, fixing the bearer of this news with a formidable stare. 'But remember if you do, I'll take this hospital down BRICK BY BRICK.'

The hospital found an alternative solution. I was playing rugby again twelve months later. My piano playing days were behind me!

Let me tell you a curious story about that school.

We were talking about coincidence and the Irish priest McEncroe being responsible for bringing my great-grandparents out from Donegal. That's not the only curious twist in this story. The first priest to be formally appointed to minister in Sydney Town, and who would build the first St Mary's Cathedral, arrived from County Cork in 1820. He was John Joseph Therry, a bit of a firebrand. Not a man who was entirely comfortable with authority, as several of the early bishops would happily attest—particularly those who were English-born. Therry was a strong personality and entirely Irish. When he died, as a result of being held in great honour by the convicts of the time (and being the beneficiary of many of their wills), Therry was a wealthy man. Much of his estate was left to fund the arrival of the Irish Jesuits to Australia.

Now, one of the coincidences that arise from this story is that part of the Therry bequest made possible the purchase of the vast estate upon which the said Riverview College stands today. Therry left one condition—that local boys without the wherewithal to meet the fees would be given free tuition. My brother and I would be two such grateful boys, thanks in part to the charming pleas of our mother. (I did describe her as ambitious, remember.)

Following the twists in the path of history is wondrous at times. 175 years after Archpriest John Therry was installed as parish priest of St Mary's Cathedral, I would find myself in exactly the same role (by then, the title Dean was used), administering the Cathedral and being responsible for his great story.

To my amazement, while I was working there, I discovered that the graves of the two Irish priests, John McEncroe and John Therry, lie side by side in the Cathedral's beautiful crypt—one brought my refugee family to Sydney; the other made possible an education for my brother and me. Someone once said, the telling of stories is necessary if for no other reason than if the story dies we can't remember who we are or why we're here. The longer I live the more certain I become of the truth of that insight.

No more Irish questions please.

Tony O'Doherty

A postscript.

Sometimes I wonder whether the friendship that has caught us both—a most unlikely friendship I must confess— might find an echo in a far off Irish village somewhere in the wild, windy hills of old Donegal. Or am I allowing that uncontrollable imagination of mine too much slack? But the Shanachie and the Priest has a ring to it, don't you think? Where can we find some compliant copper and we might set up a village?

Dear Tony,

We shall call our village McBlarney!

One day you must take me to the crypt of the Cathedral and tell me the stories. I recall it from a fleeting visit a long time ago–mostly that floor with the Celtic symbols that decorate it. It is one of those sacred secret places. Cities are full of them, aren't they? And to think it holds such an enormous part of your history–very big shoes for you to try to fill, I imagine. Perhaps you wandered down to chat to them on the days when the going got tough as Dean. Did it get tough?

NO! Don't answer that! Pack your sunscreen.

Oh, but this conversational garden path is fun . . .

Thank you for telling me about *macushla*. I feel such an idiot. All I can say in my feeble defence is that some part of me knew its meaning from the way she said it, and so I never asked. Ning always made us feel we were her darlings when we were little, and in my first year at uni I moved into her sleep-out for a time. I would creep in late and try to open the verandah door without making a sound, but it always creaked. She would call out 'There you are!', and I immediately felt safe. She never railed about the time or what I had been doing, and I, wretched youth, never amended my ways and came home earlier.

Do people still have sleep-outs? They are probably called something far more glamorous now.

I meant to say—feel no guilt at the multiple-book bedside table confession. It's the only way to read. Rather like the way a good conversation flows between friends.

And while we're changing subjects . . .

The radio is on as I write, announcing another piece of policy to chill the blood. I've been so angry about the public dialogue around asylum seekers lately; constantly put in mind of a line from *The Duchess of Malfi*. The playwright, John Webster, writing way back in 1612, says: 'a parliament is like a common fountain, whence should flow pure silver drops in general.' We're all aching for some pure silver from our own parliament, aren't we?

Hmmm. These are not thoughts for you to pack into your suitcase. No excess baggage for pilgrims.

Buen camino. Buon viaggio. Bonnes vacances. In all lingos, may you have a wonderful time. Fly high and safe, happy and healthy.

Ailsa

PS I forgot. (Sorry—no conversation ever finishes with me, does it?)

I have taken the bold step of creating a mailbox in my email program specifically for you. This is a big commitment, but not taken lightly. I feel hopeful of many years of insights and shared chat.

Travel well. I'll miss you.

DEAR READER,

Despite being crazy-busy with promoting my book and the thrill of *The Duchess of Malfi* opening at the Sydney Opera House, I missed my daily hit of Doherty when Tony went overseas. The rhythm of our letters had become a delicious punctuation to my days–though it had sped up to a mad polka by the time I opened that mailbox. I could never have guessed, even with my high hopes, how crucial our correspondence was to become for me.

Back then, I was busily working on an article or two, and a monologue for me to perform. There was plenty on my plate, you'd think, but I remember one chilly afternoon, when I was wondering where my pen-pal was, deciding to try to find a definition of 'shanachie'. There were a few, so I cobbled together the best of them. Then, out of curiosity, I looked up 'priest'. I was delighted with my findings, and I thought you might enjoy them too.

Shanachie

An anglicisation of the Irish word *seanchaî*. A traditional Irish storyteller, or bearer of the old lore.

Priest

1. An ordained minister of religion, especially of the Catholic, Orthodox or Anglican church, authorised to perform certain rites and administer certain sacraments.

2. A mallet used to kill fish when angling.

And the moral?
Fishing with priests may be something best avoided by fair-haired shanachies!
Ailsa

Ailsa,

The five-week silence is broken. The pilgrim returns from sensational days exploring Africa—Tanzania, Serengeti, Ngorogoro, Zanzibar and J'burg. My main purpose for going there was to visit Gemma Sisia, a country girl from the NSW town of Guyra, who set out to found a remarkable school in Arusha, Tanzania. In ten years it has grown from three students to 1650, twelve hundred of them boarders—entirely free of fees, three campuses. Their motto—'Fighting poverty through education'.

Richard, her husband, a Masai, is father of their four children—the last born a week ago. Our parish has involved itself in a sort of partnership to support Gemma's school for about seven years now. I thought I knew a great deal about it, but the impact of being there for ten days was astonishing. Each of the 1650 students, often malnourished, is given a substantial meal every day. A million meals a year! Gemma believes hungry children can't learn. She is a woman touched with genius, with a vision that should be bottled.

My last two days were spent in Johannesburg, really just a convenient port to exit from, but it turned into a powerful 48 hours. I found a tour guide—although this hardly describes the six-foot-six Zulu, fierce and passionate about post-Apartheid South Africa, who took four of us through Soweto, the Apartheid Museum, the houses of Nelson Mandela and Desmond Tutu, the fascinating High Court and a dozen other significant places. My Zulu guide was not to be messed with—felt a little wary about asking dumb uninformed questions, but of course, that didn't stop me bombarding him. The day left my mind reeling. I came away with the conviction that South Africa was a great country, much troubled of course, but exploding with creativity and energy. Leaves me with the sense, coming back, that here in Oz we are dawdling and quite unconscious of what is happening at this critical moment of the history of our planet. Now the bad news. I had tickets for your *Duchess* last night and came down with a heavy cold and had to give them away. Damn. The lucky recipients telephoned me this morning raving about it. You seem to see this 17th-century play raising questions we are still struggling with today. I always find that sort of historical perspective fascinating—sometimes can see the connection in old texts, sometimes it passes me by. What was it for you with the *Duchess?*

I noticed on your blog that you went to the Byron Bay Writers Festival. How was it?

Happy days.

Tony

Dear Tony,

Hooray! You are home.

Thanks for the tales. I've always been ambivalent about travelling in Africa–partly the history of Apartheid, but also an idea that the landscape might somehow feel too like Australia, when I crave otherness. I do see how stupid that assumption is, and how uninformed. To even speak of 'Africa' as one destination is so ignorant.

How is it being home? I imagine the head cold would be the least of the transitions you'd be making. Please don't worry about the *Duchess*. In the scheme of things—and hopefully in the scheme of our friendship—very small. It went well. Reviews were terrific. John Bell was a generous collaborator, and people discovered the glories of Webster's original language and imagination, which was a great pleasure for me.

T.S. Eliot wrote that Webster saw 'the skull beneath the skin'. Perhaps that's what sustained my interest. Also, of course, the Duchess herself is one of the most compelling characters in literature. Her stoicism, grace and capacity for forgiveness in the face of her own death are heart-breaking. More than anything, though, it's Webster's moral questions that draw me—not to mention the power and invention of his language and metaphors.

But why did I love it enough to devote years to it?

Who can say why love strikes? I find something new in the text every time I meet it—not unlike friendships that sneak up and surprise us. Enriching us. I'm lucky to have a few of those.

The Byron Bay Writers Festival was overwhelmingly positive. Intriguing people trying to give of their best, nuanced views, a few of my heroes, and all in the open air under golden coastal light. One of my panels was called It's Not Easy Being Good—a lively dialogue between four women about ethics and choices. I think you'd have enjoyed the conversation.

Coming home from the Festival left me appalled at the dearth of respect in our public discourse. Current affairs seems to mean shouting, posturing and grandstanding. Reading the opinion pages, I rarely find commentators who endeavour to understand the positions of the people they are rebutting. So much point-scoring, so little listening. I don't know how public figures continue in this environment, but it must be bruising. At Byron, whether by programming or luck, people were able to be the biggest versions of themselves. From what I observed, that meant that all opinions, whether in rabid agreement or disagreement, could then be heard. Perhaps people of the book are more open to hear opposing sides of a debate, but I don't think that's it. We are all capable of it, all the time. And it doesn't have to look like political correctness, or shutting down of discourse. It might just look like respect. Oh dear. Here endeth the sermon, Monsignor! Excuse me being so sanctimonious. If you could see me arguing politics with my family, you'd roar with laughter. Don't do as I do, do as I say. Please . . . Great to have you back in Oz. Send me more travel stories when you've unpacked. I love them even more than a slide night with bowls of Twisties and lashings of lemonade.

A

Ailsa,

I worry about your diet. How on earth did you walk across Spain on such fare? I can never resist the invitation to tell a story, though this one isn't from this trip. It is, however, out of Africa—and something tells me it will appeal to your sensibilities. I have often used it at weddings and anniversary celebrations . . .

In a small tribe on the west coast of Africa there is a lovely tradition.

When a woman is to give birth, the other women of the village take her out into the wilderness and together they pray, meditate and listen intently until they detect the song of the unborn child.

This small, unsophisticated and remote tribe holds the belief that the genius of every soul is in its vibration, which expresses its own unique identity. Indeed, each soul has its own song. We all have our own song.

When the women hear the song of the unborn child they sing it out loud, then return to the village and teach it to everyone else. When the child is born, the entire village gathers and sings the child's song. The first sound that the newborn child experiences is its own song.

Later, when the child goes to school, the village gathers and sings the child's song. When the child passes through the special rites of initiation to adulthood, the village gathers to sing the song. Their celebration of marriage has the man singing the woman's song and the woman replying with the song of the man. It is then that they are married. When the person comes to death, the village gathers again to sing the song.

This tribe has a unique appreciation of human friendship, and of those enduring questions: Why do we gravitate to one person rather than another? Why does a person capture our heart or mind?

Their answer—we are irresistibly drawn to those people whose song we hear. Friendship and love have much to do with recognising the particular song within the mystery of the other person. We hear their music.

Tony

Dear Tony,

Something told you it would appeal to me? What on earth could that have been? It is beautiful. And exactly how I experience friendship. Maybe a better way of describing my sense of 'knowing' someone. Hearing their song. I hope that I can listen well to yours, my new friend. My old friend. My unlikely friend. Thank you so much. Now, I have some news. It's my turn to travel. Next Tuesday I'm heading to Perth to see my dad and siblings, before flying to Ubud, where Peter and I will celebrate 25 years of marriage with ten days of listening to chooks, frogs and tuk-tuks. I will do some daily yoga practice, walk in the rice fields, sip juices and try to quiet this over-stimulated brain. We come home on the 30th August, and things are a little quieter then, I think, so I'm hoping to make some headway on the novel. Welcome home, wanderer. The days are better, knowing you are just up the road a ways.

Ailsa

PS Now that you're back, let me hit you with the big question that has been nipping at my heels while you've been away. Vocation. The calling to be a priest. How? Where? When did you know?

Ailsa,

Congratulations and blessings for your 25th. I really believe that in the right environment you can slow the racing mind. Hope Ubud turns out to be the place and August the time.

Last night I broached my dinner party question—'Can we carry the sins of others?'—led in by the travel story of my now-favourite author. What a zinger. It has led to some of the best conversations. Not without heat, of course. But a wonderful alternative to how many Olympic golds we've won/lost/ misplaced etc. What's the story of you writing a novel? You slipped that into the conversation a bit sneakily. Is there no limit to this pilgrim's creativity? Wonderful news. Your ability to climb that mountain—insight, writing skills, passion for life—is, in this little brown dog's opinion, without question.

Thinking about you celebrating 25 years with Peter in Bali reminds me that next year I'll be celebrating 50 years since I became a priest. Your question—snuck in as a postscript I note—has been asked of me a thousand times. You might find it a bit eccentric but I've probably given a thousand different answers. Mild exaggeration, but only mild.

Anyway, let me throw my mind back over those years. It was 1955—four years before you were born! I was about 22 and had been working in the corporate world for six years. Interesting enough, I guess, but I felt no real passion for it. The belief that there was 'something else' going on within me was like an itch that I couldn't scratch. I seemed to be living in a half-baked secular world that struggled to name its own spiritual longing. Something kept nagging at me, quietly and persistently, but it was not too difficult to ignore as long as I worked hard and played even harder.

One Sunday morning at Mass—I must admit a little 'tired and emotional' from a late Saturday night—I heard the story of a young man I had known at school who had joined a religious order, the Jesuits, and was now working with a nomadic group in India. He adopted their lifestyle, going barefoot, sharing their subsistence diet, sleeping rough, following their ancient rituals. His story fired me. It was like pouring petrol on to the nagging spark that I had successfully, up to then, kept protected. His story released a suppressed urge, a deep longing in me, that I felt had to be worked out one way or another. He had gambled his whole life on working for others.

To engage with the complex situations of people's lives—believing that the story of the Gospel threw its own unique light on those complexities—sounded far closer to what I wanted to do with this life of mine. I felt the compulsion to take that same bet.

The question asked a thousand times: what about celibacy? I know it might sound quite bizarre, almost eccentric in this sex-obsessed culture of ours, but the choice of a celibate life was not the game-changer that one would imagine.

Oddly, my final decision to go to the seminary, made a couple of months later, was almost taken in haste. I approached my local parish priest and eight weeks later started my studies. Lots of my most important decisions have been quite spontaneous. Taking this step was a good example. Acting instinctively often seems to work for me.

Telling friends and family was tricky. I was frightened they would laugh their heads off. Going to a seminary did not quite fit my knockabout image. My father was mystified. He didn't know what to say. My mother smiled knowingly, and quietly admitted to her friends—'Just another enthusiasm. He'll be back home soon. I'll give him two months.' My boss, at a total loss, never having faced this situation before, said, 'I don't suppose offering you more money will change your mind?' Talk about not getting it!

Trying to throw light on the reasons behind the radical choices in our life has an endless fascination for me. Why do we do what we do? It's the critical question at the heart of the science of psychology. Spirituality and psychology are closely related within the interior life of each of us. The story

I have just told you touches on a few of the reasons I became a priest. I have no doubt there are countless others, many of them arising from we know not where.

Interestingly, a similar question comes up with me when I think of you exploring a 300-year-old play to find the complex moral issues that emerge in the text, or even the more basic question of what drives you with such passion in your own writing. Sometimes the honesty and integrity with which you invest yourself in the issues you write about leaves me breathless.

So here's a challenge for you. In return for me struggling to describe to you why I have chosen such an unfashionable life's work, can you tell me why you are so passionate about the vocation of a writer? Might find, I suspect, some interesting overlap.

Not too much lolling around in the sun, drinking long, cool juices in Bali. Work please. Why do you do what you do???

Happy days.

Tony

Hello dear Tony,

Thanks for your reflection on why you entered the priesthood–and for the promise to enlarge on it. I note you hesitate to use words like vocation or calling. I guess they are what many of us might want to hear, when we pose the question to you. But life is rarely that simple, is it? 'Substantial' and 'worthwhile'. I understand those yearnings, though. We too had a visit from a missionary, when I was at school, and it moved me deeply–her selflessness. An exceptional woman. But storytelling claimed me, ultimately. It was in my bones, my inheritance, having grown up in a remote place among great mythologisers. And I note what I wrote–it claimed me, rather than me claiming it. I didn't necessarily have a 'burning bush' moment, so why should I ask for that from you? Still, I'd like to know more . . .

Now, you must be careful of these dinner party conversations. In my experience, people will start to think you are a crank! When I first mooted carrying sins for others, people looked at me as though I was barking. I hope that being a step removed–being able to say 'This loopy pilgrim did it'–will preserve your reputation as a man of some gravitas.

The novel, or whatever it is . . .

Well, it is sitting waiting for me, but I've had so little time to get back to it these past few months. I'm hoping that after our anniversary celebrations, I will get a slab of time to see what I've got.

Thanks for your encouraging words about my writing. I don't know about passion or integrity–sometimes it's just slog. Feeling a bit fragile about it this week, actually. I have to finish a piece to deliver at a fundraiser for a beleaguered Victorian TAFE college. In another cycle of government wisdom and cost-cutting, many such institutions are under threat again. Infuriating. Anyway, the event is curated by a man called Bruno, who is a whirlwind of faith in the word. He calls himself a teacher, but he's an evangelist for the power of stories to renew our lives. He has set seven writers the title *My Enduring Love Affair With Writing*. I'm finding it difficult, because I can't honestly claim that the love affair has been enduring on my part.

Well no. That isn't accurate. It has endured. It has never waned. But I have been an inconstant lover, by which I mean that as a writer, I have come and gone from writing, toyed with it and abandoned it. I have taken from it constantly as a greedy reader, and in my working life as an actor and director I've inhaled words and stories like oxygen. But I have not put back equal time and energy at the desk.

If I do think about writing as a lover, I'm reminded of that rather ghastly phrase from some Hollywood movie–'You complete me.' Well, I don't want writing to complete me. Hate the idea of that. But I'd like very much to think that I am now, finally, almost big enough to meet it. Completion I won't claim, but perhaps I needed to live five busy decades before I had grown enough to commit to writing full-time. I envy those who knew from the beginning where they lived creatively. I have been a flibbertigibbet of the first order, acting and directing and playing behind microphones and in front of cameras. Now I want to stop and do the hard, quiet, solitary yards, with 'writing' sitting quietly in the corner, perhaps growling occasionally, but mostly just waiting for me to deliver up something worthy in gratitude for all that it has given me.

Probably that makes no sense, but it is where I plan to start with the piece. I want to listen to what 'writing' wants to say. I want to write stories that are, like all of us, complicated, tender, tough, small, true, big and yes, enduring. Writing has sustained me, and so I owe it constancy and attention. The unflinching gaze. That's what I feel writing is asking of me in this phase of our relationship, so I am going to commit to it. I am going to endure with it.

I'm not sure if that can make any sense to you–or if there will be any overlap with life as a priest–but that is where the thoughts tend.

Hope you were not blown away by the winds. It is positively Arctic down here.

Only a few more sleeps until the tropics. Hooray.

Ailsa

Tony!

Greetings from Ubud! I break my silence with good news–my book is going into reprint. There is life in the sin-carrier yet! It is heaven here. Balinese bliss with a soundtrack of geck-oh! And I'm slowing . . .

Ailsa x

Ailsa,

A reprint—what a smash. In this depressed book market, that's great news. Congratulations.

Excuse me breaking into your lotus-eating time, but I have been in touch with an old mate of mine, a publisher, with whom I've been co-operating for 40 years. He is quite keen to host a discussion between us in Melbourne town about your book in late October or November, if we can find a mutual date. Could be good fun if you are game.

Wonderful to get a sense of the beginnings of your piece on the enduring love of writing.

You know, for as long as I can remember, I've been caught up with the urgency to find better words to touch people's hunger for spirituality. There is a lot of traditional religious language which is tired—a currency that has lost its original value. I love that fire in the belly that the best writers have to search for the killer sentence. I don't think it's crazy to say that we share the same drive to explore the power of language.

Now back to the lotus.

Happy days.

Tony

Hi from Lotus-land, Tony!

It's early. Pre-dawn. My favourite time. Just as the frog croaks are getting lost under the chiming of early birds, and before the whirring of motorbikes takes over, the Balinese women come into our garden. Preceded by the smoke of incense, they glide onto the verandah, placing offerings– small trays like birds' nests, made of bamboo fronds and filled with flowers, rice, fruit and little biscuits–at the door, at the family temple opposite, and at the gateway. They set them on the stone path and near the daybed. This morning, Wayan told me she makes 80 'nests' a day. The air fills with perfumed smoke as the neighbourhood is dotted with these gifts at every statue, shop entrance and tree. They are infinite in variety and contents, and they make me wonder about the offerings I make to the world–the moments when I pause in the day, as they do often, to stop and acknowledge ances-tors or history or family, or perhaps just to give thanks.

I am keenly aware, up here, of how much I have to be thankful for in my days. Not least, a new friend. Thanks for your congrats re the reprint.

I'd LOVE to have a sin-talk in Melbourne with you. I feel sure we will find something to say.

Now. A juice, I think. It took forever to one-finger tap that missive!

Selamat pagi.

Ailsa

SPRING

Ailsa,

You're back in the land of the Vegemite sandwich!

I just caught up with your blog. Every time I dip into it I get the itches: You can do that, the itch says. Then the demons of caution and procrastination scream at me: You fool! Don't take on anything more in this out-of-control life of yours. And so the chorus goes round and round.

Meeting you reminds me of a throwaway line of your favourite poet, Mary Oliver. She talks about words—chance, luck, coincidence, serendipity. But the one she chooses is 'grace'. Mary admits that she doesn't know what it is exactly, but she'll take it.

I don't quite know what it means either, Mary—but having Sandy send me your book was a graced moment.

Happy days.

Tony

Dear Tony,

At last there is time to respond properly.

Firstly, I could not be more delighted at the prospect of our conversation in Melbourne. I've written back and said I can do all the dates they propose. Yippeee!

Thank you for the reminder about Mary, and in particular for those lines and their sentiments. They are from another favourite of her poems. How lovely that you should remind me of it. I have been feeling very graced this week. A glowing newspaper review, an exquisitely designed printing of my blog post about Byron Bay Writers Festival in their magazine, thoughtful hand-written letters from readers, and a sense that the book is finding its way toward the people who will make it welcome. Truly blessings. Truly grace.

I agree with you about Sandy's role in introducing us. I think she might scoff at being thought of as an instrument of grace, or any other such highfalutin' term we could dream for her, but she most certainly is that.

This is a huge week. I'm finishing a ten-minute piece for an event called Women of Letters–a celebration of . . . well, women and letter-writing! Right up my *camino*, you would think. But among the other women writers who will be on the stage is Helen Garner–a fact that paralyses me. When I read *Monkey Grip*–way back in my late teens–I had such a shock of . . . what? Recognition? Well, yes, but no. She was living a totally different life to mine, and yet–the gift of a truly great writer–she observed particularities of her world in a way that allowed me to see, and examine, my own afresh. So much so that when I moved to Melbourne, the first thing I wanted to see was 'her' *Aqua Profonda* sign at the Fitzroy Pool. I was coming from Sydney, your city of shimmering surfaces, and moving south seemed like a pilgrimage to Helen and her deeper water.

To share the stage with her makes me long to do her justice, but the words are not flowing. It has been several weeks since I was invited to take part, and I've tried various approaches to the topic–*A Letter to my Unfinished Business*. I'm writing about my childhood home, that sheep station up in WA's Gascoyne. It makes me yearn to go back there–do you know I've not returned in over forty years? Perhaps I must finally bite the bullet. There is no question that I have unfinished business out there in that red earth. So much was lost for my parents when they left it. So much is left for me to understand. Other than that, the spirits are high, spring is in the air–and there is the prospect of excellent company in November. What more?

Ailsa

Ailsa,

So you will head north to Gascoyne country. The land where they roll their ciggies with one hand, the other casually on the saddle horn. Wonderful idea. Going back to the roots and seeing them (perhaps) for the first time. Touching my family's history in Ireland, telling the stories and singing the songs, has been one of the defining moments in my recent life. Do it. Go and see. And you, after all, are the woman who writes in her credo—'I believe that stories shape our lives.' Do send the piece you are writing if it feels right. Would love to read your impressions. And break a leg or whatever limb is appropriate for such events—but don't fall off the horse.

Tony

Hello my perspicacious friend!

You were right of course. Spending weeks wrangling at the desk, thinking and writing about my first home–the homeland of three previous generations of my family–created an itch I must scratch. So I've booked flights and will head off with Peter in a couple of weeks to search for the little blonde girl who went wandering across the dry earth, picking wildflowers. Hope she is still out there, walking.

I'll return just in time to prep for a gruelling public conversation with a Monsignor from the north. Hopefully we can plan for you to come for a meal while you're in town. I'd love you to meet Peter, and I have a couple of other close friends whose company you might enjoy. Showfolk. Your people!

Must away. It will be hot over in the north-west, and I need to pack a fly-net.

Ailsa

PS Thanks for the encouragement—or should I say, the prodding? It feels great to be on my way.

Ailsa,

Buen camino for your desert search, pilgrim. Until my early forties I had no interest in my Celtic background, despite an Irish name from a grandfather and an Irish maternal grand-mother who lived with us. Then I spent a month travelling through Ireland.

Hard to find words to describe the effect on me. The familiarity of the place penetrated depths in my psyche I never knew existed. I felt split open to a new understanding of myself. Their ironic sense of humour, their preparation of food, their music, their sensitivity to acts of injustice, their love of conversation—the Irish culture gave me an eerie sense of homecoming. It was like I saw myself anew. I was re-reading my life through a Celtic lens.

I hope your search yields similar riches.

Tony

Hola Tony!

I'm back, and of course your predictions were accurate. Huge amounts of information, memories and emotions to process. Not much I can say with any clarity just now, except that I'm grateful beyond words for the trip, and glad to be home, and well . . .

Flummoxed!

There's a word.

I have more questions than I left with, but I think maybe that is good. Now I must wash the red dirt from my clothes.

How you, *compañero*?

Ailsa

Ailsa,

Welcome back! I'm waiting for the stories and the songs. Saw the photo on the blog and was awestruck by the land. The stuff of Aussie myth. Glad you stayed in the saddle.

Probably silly to mention it, but did you see the reference to your admiration of Peter Steele, quoted by Raimond Gaita in *The Monthly* last issue? He wrote a warm reflection on Peter's life and I thought with some pride—'I know that smart, powerful and life-giving woman and damn it she walks miles and miles as well.'

Interesting. Looks like we've both been influenced by Jesuit thought. That surprised me.

If you can't find the reference I would be happy to send it.

We are all on track for our conversation. November 13/14 will be great fun.

Happy days.

Tony

Hooray!

That's wonderful news, Tony. It's in the diary.

Yes, Rai told me he was going to write about me as a student of Peter Steele's. I felt nervous at the thought of being mentioned; unworthy after not having gone to his funeral. I hadn't stayed in touch–he was very much my prof, not an intimate–and so I didn't go along to pay tribute to him. I wish I had. He impacted on me profoundly, not least because he was a real live poet. I think he would be gently amused that I'd written a travel/memoir/spirituality book, given that one of the texts I studied with him was Lawrence Sterne's *A Sentimental Journey*. He was a wise and gifted teacher, and I was fortunate to have had time with him.

You know, I never really considered him as 'Jesuit', but in hindsight perhaps it helps to explain why I was so drawn to him and his poetry–the ongoing fascination I have for anyone who can open up mysteries for me. His writing certainly did that, as did the personal conversations I managed to snatch after tutorials. A generous man.

So looking forward to seeing you again. Soon!

Ailsa

Ailsa,

Never realised how attractive as a means of communication a blog can be until I read yours. I feel selfish somehow relishing your delicious perspectives, plugging into where you are up to whenever I choose, and yet not joining the conversation. Paul Keating used to say that one is either a voyeur or a player. Hate to admit it but where you are concerned I am simply a capital V.

Enough about all that.

November is upon us.

Prepare yourself for some 'mother' stories—not sweet little *Owl and the Pussycat* stories like the ones in your book (loved them), but at the age of 94, my mother was roaring around the racecourse backing Tommy Smith's outsiders.

By the way, is the Gascoyne trip making any more sense? How did the land affect you? Do you see yourself any differently?

Happy days.

Tony

Hi Tony,

I'm amused at the idea of you as a voyeur–my blog must be the only area of your life where you can call yourself that. I know your dark secret is that you are a player who can't help but get involved. I am glad its words are resonating though.

The Gascoyne . . .

I'm not sure if sense is what will be made of that visit, but do you know, I think that it will be a writing work of some kind. Article, book, play . . . not sure which. It won't be a song, of that much you can be sure. No one needs to hear me sing!

Anyway, I had three other perspectives on the land, as well as all my own frantically scrawled notes, because I travelled with Peter, my sister Alanna, and her father.

Sorry. That's confusing.

When I say sister, I suppose I mean half-sister, though I never think of Alanna that way. She is as full as it is possible to be, and I am lucky to have her as a friend and corner-stone of my sometimes-shaky foundations.

My family is complicated–divorces and re-marriages and half-siblings. The odd thing–well, odd to other people, though it seems perfectly natural to us–is that we all get along famously and are, in spite of the ructions and eruptions of decades ago, incredibly close and protec-tive of one another. I guess that is testament in some way to my parents–all of them!–and their ability to navigate tricky emotional terrain in a way that allowed respect to be maintained. Even my father and stepfather, who were both in love with my mother, are mindful of each other, and generous with and about each other.

So there you have it—some background to the dramatis personae of the trip.

My stepfather, Frank, grew up working as a roustabout, jackaroo and manager on sheep stations, and was working on our family property when he and my mother fell in love. He, too, suffered from the loss of connection to that red dirt country that was the eventual outcome of events after the family property was sold in the divorce settlement. That landscape is part of him, and so returning was both nostalgia and a reunion.

For Alanna, who is eight years younger than me and never lived on that property, it was a chance to finally experience the physical reality of the myriad stories we had been told for decades. A place of family mythology. The fabled north-west, where everything would be right, if only we had been able to return. Not unlike the displacement stories told by refugees, except that the Gascoyne belonged to the Yamaji people before my great-great-grandparents claimed it.

But that is another layer of story. So many are swirling in my head.

Then there was me. I lived there for the first few years of my life, and have sketchy memories and many photos of me as a tot from that place.

And finally Peter, who grew up in Victoria's green rolling landscape, and for whom the Gascoyne was a revelation. Fences stretching for hundreds of miles. Endless horizons broken only by low scrub, and relentless sun overhead. Rocky, barren-seeming earth. Beautiful, yes, but how could it support sheep, he kept asking. How could anyone have thought that it was a good idea to have agriculture there?

How indeed.

It was great to share my earliest history with him and to get his take on that land after all these years spent living in, or visiting, the places of his youth.

Being in the shearing shed was the most vivid memory for me. The smell of lanolin still so strong in the noonday heat. The templates that were used to put the name of the property onto the bales–so familiar. The slotted tables for the fleeces, and the chutes beside the shearers' stations, where the sheep would scramble away after they had been shorn.

And then the creekbed. It was exactly where I remem-bered it, and that's not something I could have known from any photo. It was from that memory of toddling hand-in-hand with my grandfather, and thrilling to have it verified.

But other things were sad. The tennis court cracked and disintegrating. The vegetable gardens gone. The home fence just wires. The coolhouse walls open to the elements. The once-polished verandah–made of a mixture of cement and anthill earth–crumbling to dust. The front door boarded up because now the only entrance that is used is through the kitchen. Windmills sagging. Troughs splitting.

A kind of graveyard, really. That life is gone.

Most potent of all was one of Alanna's comments–'It's just a place.'

And it is. But it isn't.

We talked about that. About how it's also the site of stories and hopes and dreams. And so it's a place inside of us and we measure ourselves by it.

I wondered . . .

Would I have been big enough for it? Are our lives as vibrant or rich as the lives of which we were told? Will we ever know what it is to match the north?

No answers yet. Only questions. And a curious sadness. I was left with more of a sense of yearning and how that has characterised me, if not the others of my family. I should not speak for them. But I do recognise a feeling that home may be always just out of reach, and that the best part of me is somewhere else, over that distant hill. Walking . . .

Enough. I have gone on far too long. But do you know, I didn't realise any of this until I sat down to reply to you? So thanks for prompting me, Antonio. I'm grateful to have learned something. What a teacher you are for me.

Now. Nuts and bolts!

Please come to our place on the 13th. Around 7 if that suits? What a treat.

Ailsa

Dear Ailsa,

Your reflections on your return to the Gascoyne set my mind racing about the importance of the desert in the Australian imagination. Your trip to the family home, in all of its grim reality, is returning to face your lost story. It's a journey of sterling courage. You must write more about what it means to you.

There's an ancient biblical belief that the genuine prophet comes from the desert. There is also the belief that the worst of our acquisitive culture is the product of most Australians clustering around the coast, backs turned away from the mystery of this immense continent. We will only find the energy to build a future if we turn to face that mystery and find within it our deliverance. Don't waste that experience. Write about it.

Just been caught up with your book, snatching some time in a heavy day. It's simply delicious. Enjoying it all over again.

And here's a little twist! As I read, I realised I too had been in the Camino town of El Ganso—and not only that, I was in their famous Cowboy Bar! Mine was a riotous night spent with Germans who spoke no English—and my German is limited to *auf wiedersehen*. After a night of singing songs with these new friends—isn't it extraordinary how music can transcend boundaries, even the lack of language?—and being plied with Grappa by our ebullient host, I ended the night dancing with him cheek to grizzled cheek in the middle of the restaurant. Entirely disgraceful behaviour for a serious pilgrim.

Happy days.

Tony

Tony,

I've woken this morning feeling sick at heart as I hear of the latest developments into abuse within the Catholic Church. More and more I ponder your words–and wonder how you live within an institution that has failed so many, so badly. Are you coping? Do you have strategies in place? I know that faith does not lie in the Church or the clergy– that it lies elsewhere. But to have lived your life within those structures must cause enormous pain as you read of these events. I have no wish to make you speak of any of it now. Only to offer my support and a little empathy.

Much to discuss. Always. I'd better start peeling some onions for your dinner.

Ailsa

DEAR READER,

As you'll have gleaned from our letters, a Melbourne publishing house had invited Ailsa and me to speak about our separate experiences of walking the Camino, in its conference room in Mulgrave. Seemed like a good idea, even though I had only met Ailsa on that one previous occasion in Sydney. Should be fun, I thought.

On the day of the talk I was greeted by an avalanche of press headlines about the incidence of sexual abuse of children within the Catholic Church, and the issue of cover up. Photographs of George Pell, the Archbishop of Sydney at the time, were everywhere and the story of his less-than-enthusiastic response shouted out from every newsagency. I felt sick.

Here I was far away from home about to address an unfamiliar audience—as a priest, in the midst of a media firestorm.
I spent the afternoon preparing a statement about the seriously damaged victims of this abuse and about the deep
confusion that I felt. A few minutes before the programmed
talk, and with little conviction, I showed my statement to
Ailsa and our host. My speaking partner gently suggested
I jettison the prepared words and just speak my mind and my
heart. The notes were torn up.

The room was packed. A camera and lights were set up
to video stream the event. A few friends were present, but
mostly people I didn't know. To move straight into the night's
topic—the Camino—without first addressing the day's headlines, seemed impossible—and frankly, irresponsible. But
what to say?

There was nothing new for me about the issue, of course.
But the day's press barrage reopened scarcely closed wounds.
I had made such statements before—in Sydney's Cathedral,
in local parishes. This night was somehow different. Looking
carefully at the people in the intimacy of that packed room
I wondered which of them had suffered the crime of abuse?
Which of them had members of their family scarred by this

vicious epidemic? These questions always haunt me. I will never know.

And then there are the perpetrators. Sometimes the only response we can muster for such people is to lock them up and throw away the key. Take them out in a boat and drop them in the ocean. And yet there is the cruel irony that some of those worst criminals have been the hapless victims of abuse themselves. And so there is this incredible spiral of evil, circling round and round, self-perpetuating in some form of hideous spreading stain.

In this era in which the recurrence of saying 'sorry' reduces the act to cliché, how can one find language that doesn't get lost in the trite and banal, and is genuine enough to frame an authentic apology? How could I compose anything meaningful on behalf of myself, as well as those priest colleagues of mine who have crashed on the jagged rocks of abuse? Would my heart be steady enough to give birth to words honest and healing enough? My script was ripped up. I was far from relaxed.

Taking a deep breath, I confessed to my feelings of deep turmoil and bewilderment, and my utter disgust at the damage done to young people; at a wound that has crippled their lives and their sense of who they are, right into adulthood and old age. There are mid-age adults I've met whose lives have been shredded.

I spoke about my own response, and my sense of shame and inadequacy. After my effort to put these feelings into words I concluded: 'I want to express from colleagues of mine to all of you here, personally, a deep and sincere apology from my small part in the Church, entirely heartfelt, for those of you who have experienced abuse in one form or another.'

It was not perfect grammar. It was not elegant. But it was an attempt to meet people from the honesty of my own turmoil.

Eventually we directed the night's conversation to Ailsa's book *Sinning Across Spain*. What does it mean to carry someone else's sin?

Tony

Just a postscript ...

Paedophilia in our society is widespread and prevalent. The figures are stunning. It is not, I believe, a celibate disease; not a gay disease; nor a married disease. Not a male disease. Not a female disease. It is a disease pure and simple, like alcoholism. It cuts across all boundaries and it plays no favourites. It is a sickness, the effects of which cannot be understated.

DEAR READER,

The night before our public talk, Tony and his friends Justine and Paul came to dinner with Peter and me. They arrived amid much mirth–Tony had forgotten my house number, and Paul wandered up and down the street calling my Scottish name to the stars! There was, however, a more sombre moment after the introductions. Pete entertained the others while I took five minutes with Tony to speak about the shape of our talk and the announcement of the Royal Commission.

I was aware of him feeling 'out of place'. In the time since, I've witnessed the depth of his connection to his congregation and his community in Sydney. He wanted to be with them, I think–to care for them, but also to be supported by them. His sense of responsibility to them has always impressed me, as has the mutual affection I've witnessed between him and his parishioners.

Of course, he was among friends in Melbourne, old and new. And, despite everything, we laughed. The other guests were the children of his oldest friends. Paul was an actor, so there were many shared connections for us, and Justine was a warm and witty companion. The love between them was tangible in their teasing and easy banter, but I knew Tony was shaken. It was hard to see, just as it was the next night when he spoke from his heart to the audience. I admired him enormously for the way he was determined to face the issue at dinner, before and during our in-conversation and, subsequently, with his community in Sydney.

One thing that I can't agree on is Tony's contention that saying 'sorry' has become somehow ubiquitous–or devalued. My perception is entirely the opposite. Whether it be John Howard's insistent refusal to apologise to the Stolen Generations, many religious leaders' withholding of apologies for abuse, or James Hardie's protracted 'no' to asbestos victims—we are given examples on all sides, from the highest in the land, that saying sorry is not 'best practice'. It's as though something cataclysmic will ensue from a simple act of humility and responsibility. In the words of the pop singer Elton John—sorry seems to be the hardest word.

As to the statistics Tony quotes, well I have a theory there, too. I welcomed the Royal Commission. Like many people, particularly those living in Victoria where we had been mired in hearings for some time, I was keen to see the issues brought out into the open. I suspect such a commission might only ever have been possible under the prime ministership of Julia Gillard, who was not in any way beholden to a faith group.

But therein lies a twist for me. The Commission has become a kind of diversion for some. There are people for whom it has become convenient to sheet home all abuse to institutions. For as long as we can point a finger and say that this darkness exists only there, in that quarter, we can turn our eyes away from the more abhorrent fact, which is that the majority of abuse happens in family homes.

I have no idea about why or what creates abuse of children. It is unthinkable to me, wherever it occurs. But

I will not delude myself into believing that it only happens in institutions run by Catholics, Anglicans, Salvos or evangelicals or in the showbiz or sporting worlds. Or that it happens only at the hands of people of a particular sexual orientation. Abuse is happening everywhere.

I still have to strive to find compassion for perpetrators, but I hope that perhaps I'm a little more able to see some of the complexities of the issue as a result of the stories from readers of my book, and of my dialogue with Tony. Having to listen across a broken fence, to someone who appeared to be 'the enemy', has taught me much. Sometimes I wish I could take the easy option and speak of 'them and us' about abuse, but that doesn't advance anyone. Better to ask 'how and why'. At least that way there might be a chance for change. For understanding.

I love that phrase about living in hope. I still do.

Ailsa

Dear Tony,

My head is buzzing. So much to talk about after tonight.

Firstly, thank you for your gracious steering of the conversation. Also for accepting my suggestion to ditch the reading you'd prepared, and to speak from your heart. Your humility, confusion, and sorrow spoke more directly than any received wisdom might have. I don't think people were ready for considerations of the future. It was a relief to hear someone from within the Church speak without spin. I was grateful for that, and was moved by the ensuing conversation, and by the personal stories people told me afterwards.

So much grief and damage.

Fly safe. And thank you again for instigating something that was so affecting—and useful, I hope. My great wish, to be useful.

I didn't expect to sleep tonight, but I think a shift occurred by virtue of sharing stories, and now I'm longing for the pillow.

Hope your eyes close.

Ailsa

Dear Tony,

I'm looking at a photo of us in conversation, sent to me after last night—you in full flight in your pink shirt and me gazing at you with rapt attention!—and I'm reminded of how much our meeting has meant to me. I still have that feeling of having known you before, even though I am conscious you are new to me.

I trust you will make quiet time for yourself. I was acutely aware of your pain and 'confusion'—as you named it.

It didn't look like that, and doesn't show in the photo, but one never knows what is inside another.

I will be taking long walks this weekend. Three days, three to five hours each day. I will walk with you in my thoughts.

Ailsa

Ailsa,

Firstly, the touching and precious gift of the *camino* shell you collected at Finisterre, accompanied by your lovely note. Thanks. It was the perfect conclusion to an exceptional night. (I will beat down the frisson of guilt that rises in me that I arrived empty-handed.)

Ailsa, your elegance of mind and breadth of heart made a great impact on everyone there—no less than on your oh-so-fortunate conversation partner. I felt so much 'at home' with you sitting on my little Andy Williams stool. And the readings were riveting.

Feeling a little brittle this afternoon. But that too will pass.

Happy days.

Tony

PS The new blog post is thoughtful (as usual) and full of insight.

Dear Tony,

I'm relieved you are home and will take a breather. I've been glad to retreat into my cave. I found our night energising, but also enervating–the push-pull of the extrovert exterior and introvert interior, coupled with the stories I heard.

Now . . .

No guilt frissons, please. The impulse to give that shell to you rose from a sense that our connection is important for me, and because it came via the Camino, that holy and unholy road.

Thank you for your generous words. I think we shared an intention for the night, and were prepared to look after each other and, where possible, everyone else in the room. Yes, exactly–'at home.'

Put your slippers on and pop your feet up. But avoid the pipe.

Ailsa

Ailsa,

No slippers tonight. No pipe ever.

A little sobering, but sometimes it seems my life is surrounded by dead and dying people. And do you know, being with them is often strangely satisfying?

I think that the reason for this is that the tradition I come from, the literature which is important for me, takes death seriously.

This morning a woman came to the door with her husband. Her 94-year-old father had just died—fifteen minutes ago. He'd been sitting up large as life last night watching the footy with his son. This morning dead.

Coming to the hospital, I anointed him. His family was there—five of them. We prayed. We talked about him. We sat round the bed. My feelings were of having a strong connection with the members of the grieving family. It was deeply human. Cuts through the other stuff that we pay so much attention to. It's balancing somehow.

Despite the immense varieties of belief, and the different reactions to the death of a parent, or anyone I suppose, I get the sense that prayer works.

These are words I sometimes use in a funeral service:

Sometimes I wonder what prayer really is.
Well, here's a couple of things that it is not ...
Prayer is not the fashioning of unfamiliar, stumbling words to a distant God;
Prayer is not some form of magic
or merely the delusions of a frightened people
Prayer is actually a form of loving.
It is a rich juicy language of love.
Love of the astonishing gift of this planet
Love of the people who have touched our lives
Love of the mystery that has given us life and embraces us
Throughout our journey.

To leave a father happily caught up with a football match one minute, dead the next morning ...

There is something cruel about it. To be with a parent when they die may be scarifying, but it is also sacred. To have been with both parents as I was is, I imagine, quite rare.

Dad died in a veterans' hospital aged 75.

At the age of nineteen, a boy from Broken Hill, he had volunteered to slog through the mud and the blood of France in 'the war to end all wars'. In the bitter Australian campaign to regain Villers-Bretonneux, Dad's field artillery piece was struck by an enemy shell, knocking him unconscious and leaving him with a mild but continually irritating speech stutter.

Six months before he died, he suffered a cerebral stroke, and entirely lost his ability to speak. An earnest young therapist, ignoring the clear evidence that he only had a few weeks to live, took on the seemingly futile task of helping him regain his speech. She employed the therapy of song to restore her patient's voice.

When I visited, Dad would greet me with a dazzling smile like a passing car with lights on high beam, quite unlike the man I'd known. But more to the point, one morning he greeted me with a song he had learned as a WWI digger all those years before—'Mademoiselle from Armentières'.

He was irresistible. Lazarus coming from the tomb … singing!

Don't tell me miracles can't happen. The care and belief of this young woman therapist gave us one. A gift to his wife and children in the last days of his life, never adequately able to be repaid.

The singing digger died at night. Mum and I were next to him. His last battle was to breathe. His body fought to the last gasp. The song ended. The old digger slumped and left us.

His wife of 45 years lowered her head on to his chest and broke down in grief. I had only infrequently observed any demonstrations of affection between them, and so I was taken aback by the passion of her response. It was beautiful. My own sobbing rose up from some primitive part of my body, never before visited.

Mum lived on, placing bets, sipping whisky and squeezing every last drop from her days. She died in her 99th year.

Those decades after Dad died were as packed as a bulging suitcase returning from a trip away. A woman of remarkable energy matched by a determination for life that would make an Olympic athlete pale. Her capacity 'to party' as kids say today, had no limits. She made friends wherever she went. In her nineties, at her frequent visits to a Sydney racecourse, she held court over her own circle of punters, mostly men, under a tree close to the Tote betting window.

The last couple of weeks of her life were spent in a small sunny room with the Little Sisters of the Poor, a religious order of nuns who define gentleness. Who will replace them when they depart this city, a place that at times can be as tough as teak?

The sister taking care of her called me.

'She hasn't got long to go, Father.'

Leaving my desk, I grabbed a toothbrush and razor, and moved into her room on a mattress on the floor. Mum was not conscious, I thought—breathing from some shallow place, but not uncomfortable. Being with her brought a swirl of emotions, but strangely not all grief-laden. There was a deep feeling of being secure, somehow.

Strange at such a time. That feeling of holding your own mother, who had been the source of so much of life's rock-like security, while at the same time being acutely aware of the many times those very roles had been dramatically reversed.

But the memories—ah, the memories!

A little chap, cuddling her leg while a violent thunderstorm broke overhead, I can still feel the rough texture of the plaid skirt she was wearing. Hanging out the family washing on a windy, sunny morning—realising the difficulties associated with pegging out large sheets in the wind. Having her correct my diction in a city department store—not yeah, but YES Mummy! Insisting that I learn to play the piano, in the teeth of my equally stubborn resistance.

I prayed. God, I prayed!

I prayed with her as her breathing became a gentle mantra. I prayed for her with the deepest prayer of thanks that I could ever remember fashioning. I prayed the Office of the Dying—'We shall dance and rejoice in your mercy, Lord. We shall never hope in vain.'

I just sat and held her hand through the night.

The morning sun splashed through the window. I felt our relationship, as mother and son, as never before. Someone brought me the morning paper, and as I sat reading, distracted by some story of cricket, a nun came to the door with a cup of tea.

'I think she has slipped away, Father.'

The stupidity of it all. She quietly left this world while I was idly glancing at the sports page. I comforted myself with the belief that her Celtic sense of the absurd would have left her with a long-suffering smile of resignation, so familiar to me, knowing the son she had raised even better than he knew himself. Ignoring her, blissfully, with my head in a newspaper.

I don't think that death, or at least the death I encounter professionally, makes me sad. But it sure makes me reflective. And, a faint hope ... a little more human.

Think I'll get into my *camino* shoes and do some walking this weekend in sympathy, or empathy, or some other connect-ing thingy.

Not sure how to finish this. Perhaps with a full stop.

Ant

Hi Tony,

I guess death is the big full stop, isn't it? And the memories have certainly made you reflective. I am the beneficiary today and my inheritance is the gift of your stories. Thank you so much. How could you possibly become 'more human', I ask myself. What could that mean?

You are right about the privilege of being present to farewell a parent. Mum's death was not particularly easy–they had to manage the pain, and at only 57 she still had several lives to live–but I have always been profoundly grateful that I was there with her during those final days. It was right somehow, even if it felt deeply wrong to me at the time. I wasn't angry about it I don't think, but I did have a strong feeling that it wasn't just. She had such a capacity for life, when so many people seem to hang on a long time, not wanting to be here and not valuing their days. But such thoughts are pointless. A waste. She went with a kind of honour that I loved.

I think I understand what you say about death balancing the other stuff of the week. It's impossible to live constantly with that visceral awareness of mortality and the clarity about priorities that we feel when we lose someone, but there is no doubt that death can bring gifts to the living, when and if we are able to see them. It's much easier when someone has had a long and full life, I think. Your perspective on it is different to mine—how not, when you are so regularly with people at the end, or at funerals?—but I sense some common ground, too.

My first close experience of death was at seventeen, when a girlfriend died of bone cancer. It was a sharp lesson for all her friends, particularly because back then the treatment was quite harsh. One of her legs was amputated. She was a beautiful creature. A kind of angel, but with mischief in her. I still think of her when I hear that Simon and Garfunkel song 'Cecilia'–she did a dance performance to it, lighting up the stage and all who watched her.

I lost a lot of friends in my twenties–overdoses, anorexia, and then the big one, HIV/AIDS. One day, when I have time to write it properly, I'd like to tell you about my funny friend, Greg. He died a year and a day after my seemingly unstoppable mother. I was with them both, doing some of the practical stuff that bodies need when they are letting go, in the lead-up to their deaths. I was lucky to be there.

I've often marvelled that although I've been around a lot of death, I've never seen a human birth. People tell me that's a shame, and I'm sure they are right, but I think death can be beautiful. Some find that a macabre or weird thing to say, but I have seen astonishing things, in myself and others, at the end times. I've seen people rise and rise.

I'm sorry, Antonio, I must dash. I hope that the grieving family continue to hold each other–and to pray in whatever way is right for them. I've often looked to sunrises and sunsets and inky night skies at such times–and at the new growth on burned tree trunks, and the birds' nests that survive. I am reminded of mystery, and comforted by new life. Doesn't necessarily stop the tears, but they are my prayers, and they are solace of a kind.

And while I think of it–why do we use the expression 'reduced to tears'? What does that imply about us? I never think someone is smaller, or less, because they weep, and mostly, if I have been brought to tears, I am healed by letting them flow. Reduced? I don't think so.

I'm up at our shack in the goldfields. We've had this block of land for 23 years. It's twelve acres of pretty stony ground, with a cedar kit-home and a dam. Sounds ordinary, and I guess to most other eyes, it is–but every inch of it has been worked over by Peter and me. Well, mostly Peter. He rakes and burns and digs. We have both carried rocks and pulled out acres of weeds, almost every year. We've mowed and mowed with his old Victa push-mower. And we have shared it with friends . . . so many friends . . .

But today it is just us and the wildlife–of which there is plenty. Magpies and kookas and wee wrens calling to Pete as he piles up fallen branches for bonfires. Meanwhile, I have a pot of rhubarb, apple and ginger cooking for tomorrow's breakfast, before I set off to walk my legs into the ground. Oh, the ground, the earth, the road. On Sunday and Monday I plan to walk more and to write while Peter will clear and burn in prep for the summer season. Rural days. A blue wren is tapping furiously at the window–a little crosspatch telling me to get on with life because it won't wait for me.

See what I mean about prayers? That's another, right there.

Here's to sympathy, empathy and connecty things!
Ailsa

Ailsa,

Rhubarb for breakfast? Don't you know anything about sensible diet? Remember—you're talking to a 1950s man. Porridge for breakfast and rhubarb at night.

I like the way you interrogate language. You're right about 'reduced to tears'. Where did that come from? And why are men not allowed to cry? Or is it that we are not capable of crying? An echo of parental advice in the half-forgotten childhood?

Some claim it's not sex or survival that fundamentally drive us, but our efforts to continually try to please our mothers. For some of us old enough to have been affected by it, it may be the necessary repression that came from living through war.

Whatever its source, there is a fully equipped sentry in many of us, standing guard over the gate that allows men's emotions to pass through—above all, the human emotion that displays tears in public.

Here's a bit of theory for you, shanachie.

I once heard—the idea has never left me, really—that we all carry heavy saddle-bags of distress. They weigh us down. Distress is an accumulation, sometimes over many years, of grief and hurt. Even caused by events that we seem to have long forgotten. Lost loves, bitter criticism, frequent put-downs, relationships we have mucked up, times we have disappointed ourselves—all manner of things leave us with what could be called distress. It sits inside us, not budging, like stones in the gall bladder. It eats at our capacity to love, our ability to say what we mean, it can even take the zest out of life.

As little kids, we knew intuitively how to rid ourselves of this distress. Two ways. Firstly, crying. Little kids cry easily, they even throw tantrums. Secondly, they claim the attention of another person, often their mum.

Sadly, as we grow, we are discouraged from crying—not just men, by the way. There are real constraints on women as well, I know.

And to receive the unqualified attention of another in these grossly distracted days, is a rare event. This theory adds an interesting twist to the universal lack of people who will genuinely listen to us—it holds that the one we seek attention from is blocked by their own weight of distress.

So, to be denied the opportunity to weep, or to deny yourself the freedom of tears, may have deeper ramifications than at first recognised. Tears do not reduce, they have the capacity to irrigate our spirit, our heart and our mind for a fuller, more liberated life.

And after all those wise-sounding words, I still cringe when I imagine myself shedding tears. One memory sums me up . . .

It was at Michael's funeral. He was 90 years of age. 'Not a bad innings,' we consoled ourselves. He had been the parish priest at Maroubra for fifteen years, after quietly working away in other places for over six decades with his gentle human touch. He had an unnerving resemblance to Alfred Hitchcock—rotund, little turned-up nose, fairly bald—but it was the waddle that nailed it.

I loved him. Loved him like a son loves a father.

We had been working together for the last ten years. Lovely relaxed relationship of mutual respect thinly disguised in the familiar male manner of never losing the opportunity of 'slagging' one another.

There's another behaviour that will set you wondering, I know. Already I can hear you mulling over why it is that we show affection by disparaging those we love. It's the Irish in us, some claim.

Anyway, as we placed his casket in the hearse, I was totally swept away with tears. Not just wet eyes, but uncontrolled weeping, wracking sobs coming from I knew not where. That's not the way it should be, I told myself. I'm a priest. Funerals are an important part of my ministry.

Accompanying the deep grief of others is such a familiar experience for a priest, that a tough skin can grow over natural feelings. However regrettable it may be to admit it, it helps to hold some 'professional' distance, they say.

This particular morning, none of those rules applied. I was awash. I was embarrassed, and also embarrassed at being embarrassed. I looked for some corner away from the gaze of the dozens outside the church. Big boys don't cry. Priests have to have broad shoulders to support others, don't they?

An old Jewish saying holds that what soap is for the body, tears are for the soul. Well, Michael's final gift of friendship to me was the treasure of passionate tears. They reminded me that we can't distance ourselves from life, or from grief. Those tears enlarged me.

Tony

Dear Tony,

'That's a good girl. You just sit there and have a good cry.'

I remember being told that as a little girl by my grand-parents and by elderly nuns and by Mum and Dad and aunts and . . . well, everyone. I don't know if my brothers were given the same message.

As I got older, I did begin to feel embarrassed by tears—to associate them with weakness. But nonetheless, I can still let them fall when they insist. And I'm glad I can. I'm not a weeper, but boy do I understand, in my cells, the release they bring. The change. And yes, the expansion.

Thanks so much for the story of your Michael. He must have been quite a man.

Now, to change the tone, pilgrim . . .

I'm writing to you out of left field! It's looking like I may come to Sydney for a flying visit very early next Friday morning, and leave on Sunday. Any chance of a sighting?

Ailsa

Great news!

Saturday morning for coffee or lunch—I have a wedding at 3 pm—or late afternoon 4/5.30, is fine. Sunday is a somewhat crowded day.

You'll recognise me from my walking sandals and my staff.

Tony

PS Have you heard the saying that there are three things that can cure anything—sweat, tears or seawater. All of them salt.

I think it might be true.

Dear Tony,

Yippee! 11 am on Saturday will be grand. I'm staying in Lewisham and need to be in Elizabeth Bay at 1 or 1.30, so that gives us plenty of time. I'd suggest a mini-*camino*, but won't have my boots–or a staff, sadly. We will have to make do with city sitting. I await instructions!

And now I might go and sweat around the block in celebration.

Ailsa

PS You wrote–'Sunday is a somewhat crowded day.'

Ha ha! Funny man.

But tell me, out of interest, what does a typical Sunday usually involve?

Ailsa,

Sunday in the trenches—would you seriously like to know?

It's busy with people and events, but it always comes with a buzz. We have three masses here at Rose Bay and a Saturday afternoon mass at Dover Heights. Five or six hundred people. Then there will be two or three baptisms after the 10 am service. They will bring their own gang. It's never dull. Kids everywhere.

When you make contact with that number of people then the stories begin to flow—a mother has just died overseas; a child has been diagnosed with leukaemia; a marriage has broken up; another couple want to arrange a wedding. As I get older, I try to hold Sunday afternoon to be quiet and people-free. Sometimes it works!

Now. Here's the plan.

I can pick you up at the exit at Redfern station at 11 am Saturday (or any time earlier, say 10.30 if that suits—but I'm really just being greedy).

How does that sound?

Tony

Hi Tony,

Be greedy! I'm completely thrilled that it has worked out for us to have time. The more the better–and hopefully merrier. Though I'll try not to suck up too much of your oxygen before that busy Sunday of yours.

It seems mad for you to come to Redfern. I can easily take the train from Lewisham to the city, then swap to the Eastern Suburbs line and alight at Edgecliff. Wouldn't that be easier? What say you, dear local?

Ailsa

OK, Edgecliff sounds good.

Why are you so much smarter than a burnt out parish priest?

See you under a big tree.

Antonio

Querido Antonio.

You are not burnt out and you have strict instructions not to get burnt out. We have a *camino* to walk! Just make sure your mobile is on. I've seen you in digital action and it's not reassuring.

Ailsa

Me again, Tony.

Amazing to think it is only a week since our talk in the bookroom. To me it feels like about ten lifetimes. It must be even more pronounced for you. I can't imagine how things are in your community with the abuse revelations, but I'm guessing you will be doing a lot of comforting. A wedding will be good this weekend, I imagine. Some optimism and promise?

Anyway, I wanted to say I'm thinking of you and hoping the days are not too hard. Also to say I'm glad to be seeing you again so soon.

Until Saturday. Keep well—on all levels.

Ailsa

Damn it woman. We're doing it again.

Emails passing in cyberspace. Yours arrived just as I was about to press send.

Sure you are not a Celtic witch?

Anyway, here goes ...

Ailsa,

The only reason to send you these reflections when I will see you on Saturday is that I need to put some of it down in note form. Also, let's be frank, I might forget to tell you some of these things. You're dealing with some sort of major eccentric here, y'know.

So, to the week that was ...

Wednesday night last. Loved it. Sitting up on those stools and chatting so comfortably. Being intoxicated once again by the road and its memories. My intoxication fuelled by the lightness and yet intensity of your prose, but this time brought to another level by your reading of it.

All of these feelings being torn open and nerves exposed by the terrible realities of the abuse of children. And yet the fun and memories of the road were strangely undiminished. And finally my enthusiastic public promise: 'And damn it I'll walk the Camino again.' No need to hit the alcohol or drugs for me to get high.

Then the afterparty. And you saying to me (in the same intoxicated state, I believe), 'Let's do the Camino together.' You may have noticed I just managed to maintain sufficient control of the seventeen-year-old adolescent who wears the disguise of mature aged cleric and my hasty and enthusiastic tongue—not to reply. Then to have the night capped off by your astonishing gift and note. Your treasured shell.

Which brings me to the point. Opening the box to proudly show to my hosts, I was visited by disaster. It slipped out of my fingers and fell on the wooden floor AND BROKE. The shell you safely carried from Finisterre to the plane, from the plane to your home, cherished for two years, and then gave to this clumsy pilgrim, fell to the ground and broke. My overloaded emotional system was hit as if by 240 volts of electricity. I stared at the pieces on the floor, aghast.

The good news is that it has been restored to almost unrecognisable wholeness with the care of a watch-maker and the judicious use of Araldite by my wonderful hostess.

How can I tell Ailsa, the truth-teller? The coward's way—email.

When facing crises like this I regularly turn to metaphor.

The delicately beautiful shell—is your story, your grace and curiosity, the written word of the book, the love affair with walking, the life-giving friendship you offer us dusty fellow pilgrims.

The disaster—is the brick wall of horror of the abuse and the deep wounding of the innocent, the smashing of lives. The waters of sin that threaten to drown us.

The reconstruction—the fragile possibility of reconciliation, of putting lives together, the healing power of stories, the surprising mystery of strangers we meet on the way.

I don't know whether it works for you, but it seems to take some of the sting out of it for me.

Thursday night. Spoke to about two hundred people in Albury. Made a similar statement to the night before. The topic was the possibility of connections that a community of faith offers us, and which we often fail to recognise. The audience was kind. Led to intelligent and worthwhile discussion.

Friday morning. Came home a little stretched. Had a meeting of six of my colleagues, all good men, equally flattened by the week's headlines. All dealing with it in their own different ways. *Paso a paso*.

Friday afternoon. Out of the blue I get a phone call from an Italian woman. I can hardly make out what she wants—but she needs to come and see me at 5 pm. Of all times, of all weeks, of all days it turned out to be a party of wild Italians from Bolzano, one of whom I had met on the Camino at Ponferrada three years ago. The afternoon turned into another extravagant *refugio* experience. Lucio Perenzoni from Salerno and five of his *amici*, out in Oz observing the eclipse of the sun in Cairns. No English. My Italian disappears when not in use for any length of time. So it's all mime, huge hugs, high fives, immense smiles, laughing without reason, talking extra loudly. Sentences of one word. Either Latin, Italian or something I've heard in the movies. Lots of photos. It goes on for an hour and a half. They leave yahooing, much tooting of the taxi horns. Passers-by think I have just been married but they can see no bride.

Later that night—a fiftieth birthday, full of loud music and thin conversation. I leave at 1 am to find my car battery flat—or is it *my* battery.

An incredible week comes to an end.

Gracias a la vida.

Tony

Dear Tony,

What highs and lows. I'm very relieved there were highs. And the Camino rescued you of course–those mad Italians.

They are infectious in that fizzing state. I know it well. Italy was my first love. My first trip outside of Australia. I'll never get that curious mix of homecoming and unfamiliarity again–although funnily enough, that's how I felt when I met you, now I think about it. Anyway, I experience a shimmer of that initial visit to the northern hemisphere whenever I speak Italian, or listen to them bubbling. How kind that they descended on you. You were healed by the Camino–or am I projecting for my own reasons!

The shell . . .

Your metaphorical reading of its journey will always be there now, when you see it. That visceral experience of the day, the week, the breaking open.

Before reading your interpretation, I'd formulated a version of the significance of the smashed shell–clearly, I thought, we have to walk to Finisterre so you can get a replacement!

As to me being a witch–which you have asked several times, I note . . .

That word has had a very bad rap. Did you know that it was originally applied to both men and women? These days it is either a sexy young thing or a hag on a broomstick–kind of a broad-strokes distillation of the way much of our culture wants to portray women. I don't know anything about the practices of Wicca, but I suspect many people who are drawn to it would be offended by society's over-whelming view that 'witch' is somehow associated with malevolence or darkness.

I don't get the sense you are using it that way. Quite the opposite. I rather suspect you're revealing your fascination with all things Celtic. Regardless, I will take it as a compli-ment, and claim a little witchiness for myself. I actually love the word 'crone'. I often use it of myself, and people are horrified. To me it's almost an aspiration—the wise woman who retreats to the cave. And do you know, it has the same derivation as 'crown' which makes me think it was a word for a priestess? Take care or I might move into your terri-tory, Monsignor!

I'm glad you are pieced together like the shell after such a time of breakage. All shall be well. And all manner of things shall be well . . .

Ain't it the truth—given time?

Ailsa

Compañero!

I dreamed about the shell overnight. Do you recall I decided to give you the perfect one and to keep the chipped one for myself. Did I tell you that? Well, now we both have fault lines! There's something in that for me to understand. Something about allowing everyone to be broken. Not projecting perfection onto those I care about and admire, because it's an impossible burden for them to bear.

How a metaphor opens the world.

A

A

Some singer or other talked about the light coming through the fault lines. I like that. This search for perfection—I got over it years ago. I'm happy with the cracks.

I like Saturdays, and this one promises to be no exception.

T

DEAR READER,

The distance from Melbourne to Sydney is roughly a thousand kilometres. For my Shanachie friend, that's little more than a stroll!

I often feel an urge to explore why Ailsa is such an incessant walker. Walking surely is an exercise that demands little justification. The natural movement of a healthy human body. Fresh air, stretching legs, breathing deeply—all worthy activities that make good sense. But walking 1300 kilometres, alone, through flooded rivers and icy weather while carrying all your possessions in a heavy backpack from one end of Spain to the other—now that IS a question that invites some serious discussion.

Why do we do what we do?

For me, an endlessly intriguing question. It pointed me toward reading psychology. What really makes me tick? It had me looking carefully at the stories of my own parents, their parents and their parents' parents—as far as I could dig. Maybe I could find clues there.

As you've already heard, about 30 years ago I stumbled on the story of my own Irish background, which has shone a partial light on some of my choices. So I was delighted when, in a quick aside, Ailsa told me the intriguing story of her great-great-grandfather John Bernard's multiple journeys from Fremantle to the Gascoyne—a distance of 1200 kilometres. No trains, no boats—simply hard slog.

The story in a nutshell . . .

Irish-born Bernard Fitzpatrick arrived in 1851 to start a new life in Australia. Thirty-one years later his son, John Bernard, set out from Fremantle on a highly ambitious journey to stake a claim in the red dust of the Gascoyne plains of Western Australia. The motivation for this journey is not hard to find—the irresistible lure of land, vast tracts of land, that drove new settlers, particularly the Irish and the Scots, to set out with only a pack full of hopes, into the hinterland of this immense continent.

The terrain must have appeared incredibly harsh to his Celtic eyes. But he stayed. Not before, however, returning to Perth to formalise his claim, then retracing his steps back to the Gascoyne where he'd spend two years alone readying the property. Then, finally, he trekked south *again* to collect his wife and six children, his goods and chattels, to bring them at last to their new home.

John Bernard was already a prodigious traveller who had crossed from the UK to Australia three times in a sailing ship before he was twenty. We are talking about a man who, beyond any shadow of doubt, was a restless pilgrim. But here is the fascinating parallel—that journey to the north was roughly the same distance that Ailsa would walk from the south to the north of Spain, over a hundred years later. Don't tell me that genes have got nothing to do with it.

Wrinkles are hereditary. You get them from your kids—so goes the old saying. Our inheritance, our personal history and our genes, I am convinced, play a significant part in the way we look at the world, the choices we make, the friendships we fashion, our patterns of health and wellbeing, even the journeys we embark on. Which brings me back to the not surprising insight into what drives this contemporary restless pilgrim who carries the genes of her ancestors and their epic journeys as they built a future in the timeless spaces of North Western Australia.

The Gascoyne would be the desert in which the infant Ailsa would take her first steps.

Tony

Buenos dias, Antonio!

I've had a great Sydney visit. Rich encounters and wonderful conversations.

None more so than ours. Didn't we roam!

Hope your Sunday is full-fill-ing.

Thank you again for great gifts. I'm glad I can now picture where you will be reading this. Next time you visit Melbourne I will show you my office eyrie!

Gracias. Always *gracias, compañero.*

Ailsa

Ailsa,

You never told me what *compañero* means to you. For me, it's one with whom you break bread, with whom you break open your life.

One of the many little corners we failed to explore.

Been thinking about your jokey use of the label 'blonde', and how I said I didn't like you using it, even in jest. It diminishes you, as most labels do. I have to tell you I'm actually not too keen on them. Comes from my constant irritation at people seeing me simply as 'priest' and then quickly drawing all sorts of false assumptions about what I believe, what are my values and opinions about all manner of things. Their suppositions are consistently wide of the mark. Gives me the irrits.

When you tell me you are 'blonde' I think you're saying you embrace innocence, don't want to be seen as an expert, or having the last word—easier to be the person who is not afraid to ask the 'dumb' question, which is the one everyone else is wanting to ask. I get that. Let me tell you, however, my feisty sister Susie is a blonde and she wouldn't fail to cut me to pieces if I attempted blonde jokes with her. Here endeth the second sermon on the matter.

Fancy me forgetting I had that baptism date on Saturday and losing those precious conversation minutes. Must confess that it is far from unusual for me to double book, even triple book myself. I should wear a health warning on a T-shirt perhaps—'man out of control'.

When I get excited like this, I have to remind myself of a theory of group dynamics I once learned. It talks about three stages within the pattern of most relationships: 'enchantment', followed by 'necessary disenchantment', before coming to 'mature consolidation'. If that is simply gobbledegook to you remind me to talk about it some fine day.

Whatever about all of that, I think we are in the good times at the moment. We might be heading for stage two. Look out.

One sobering thought niggles at me—your generous openness in embracing a dialogue with someone engaged in a more and more discredited profession these days, as the endless stories of abuse roll on. I imagine some of your friends counselling you to consider seriously before taking on a correspondent who has all the breathless appeal of some sleazy drug dealer. The image might be a little strong of course, but you know what I mean.

I hope you realise how good it was to spend time with you—little though it was. I feel quite powerful connections. I am gripped by the turns in the journey, and all that has happened since Easter. Hope I can keep up with this pilgrim who has fallen into stride with me. I find you a delightfully easy person to feel 'at home' with.

Thanks.

Tony

Hello again, Antonio!

I'm in another world. I drove from the airport up to our shack in the country to meet Peter. We are now sweltering in 30-plus heat with impossibly large flocks of cockatoos and crows overhead. We're perplexed, never having seen such numbers of them in our 23 years of coming here. Maybe there is something dead nearby, or maybe it's the three years of good rains that have changed the country-side and made it more delectable to birds, 'roos and all wildlife. There are even more snakes about this year. I've seen one almost every weekend recently when I've been out striding.

Anyway, aside from the squawks of birds and the cicadas chirruping, all is quiet. Oh, no—there's the clunk-clunk of a wooden wind chime, souvenir of a trip to Bali twenty years ago, back in the days before fake designer watches.

Silence sprawls. It's both settling and unsettling after the swirl of faces that was—and always is—my experience of Sydney.

'Compañero.'

Yes, you have it in one! *Com*–'with'. *Pan*–'bread'. It's our English word, companion, of course. Something much deeper and more tribal than *amigo*, in my lexicon. I use *amigo* of many people—and in the case of the *amigo* in my book, it was used consciously to remind me and readers that he was 'friend' and not *amante*–'lover'. Sometimes a label can help, you know. But '*compañero*' has music in it, and that notion of breaking bread suggests time and silence spent together, something deeper and of the spirit. And yes, I'm aware of the biblical overtone and am very peaceful with it.

So. *Compañero* . . .

There you are!

Labels and names are particularly tricky in the area of relationship, I think. Once, 'companion' was a euphemism for lover, particularly for gay couples. Now we scoff at it as old-fashioned or coy, but in some ways I think it is perfect. I certainly prefer it to partner. Or to 'wife', now I think of it. That can have overtones of ownership, though mercifully, my marriage has never had any sense of that for me. 'Companion' has resonances that appeal enormously.

'Friend' seems to me to be the greatest compliment one can give anyone. I believe it comes from a Germanic root, which it shares with the word 'free', and the meaning of the root word is 'to love'. I used to say that if I could choose my epitaph it would read 'She was a good friend'. Peter and I are friends—we are companion-able together, too. I'm proud of that. We can share silence, and I travel more easily with him than with anyone else—sure signs!

Loving well is a life's work, isn't it? We get so caught up in categories and labels, and in the complexity of that over-used, over-valued, de-valued word 'love'. It always seems to me that the heart doesn't have an appetite for categories and language. Its job is just to feel. The mind wreaks havoc with the heart, trying to tell it what it can and can't feel, and about whom, and what age they must be, or what gender. The heart knows only that its job is to expand and love. Wherever it can. It does it with such ease and . . . well, grace.

It's grace that you and I got to find each other, I think. Grace bathes every meeting of a like mind, and every hard-won relationship. I find it incredible that humans get to love each other—and in such a variety of ways.

By the way, I don't mean some wafty, misty-eyed touchy-feely romantic thing, either. Love is the most active verb I know. It is putting oneself out to accommodate another, it is sitting by a deathbed, making soups and cakes, holding a hand, picking up pieces.

And it is writing letters, you know, Tony. Responding, when tired or confronted. Turning up, when a question irritates or touches nerves. Extending, making time, straining to understand another. Co-responding. Letters are a kind of loving. Call them correspondence or call us pen-pals—what we've been doing is opening our hearts as well as our minds, and that takes effort.

Funny.

People throw the 'love' word around about the most vacuous things. I do it. 'I love rhubarb,' I will say–though let us not underestimate the mighty rhubarb–or 'I love red nail polish'. But when the verb 'to love' is used for something real and true, something hard-earned, we are afraid to use it.

I don't dispute that there are different kinds of love, but I do wish people would own up to it more truthfully about the big things. I would be appalled at myself if any of my home village ever doubted that I love them–if I had not been generous enough to tell them. One of my fears is that I could die leaving anyone I love in doubt as to my feelings for them.

Of course I do see there are easy and hard loves. I think the most demanding is with the husband, wife, partner, companion–the one who has to do the day-to-day turning up of domestic life. From the dropped towels to the shared terrors of health scares; from the coping with another's family to the ache of their disappointments or frustrations; from the grind of routine to the ever-present gas bills–Hollywood and company rarely acknowledge such things, and most friendships don't ask it.

Look at us. We are not face to face. We get to choose when to turn up to each other. Which bits to reveal and which to erase—aren't you grateful for that 'delete' button? We don't have to manage each other when tired or grumpy or broken—your word. We can present our Facebook faces. We only have to answer to each other in time, rarely in space, as we did (with such happiness, can I say?) this weekend.

I'd still argue that there has been a cost, at least in time and thought and willingness to engage. We have made something already, you and I, and it is formed out of a kind of love, that most demanding noun and most active verb.

Good grief. So much more to write in reply to you, and I have gone off on a tangent, as I often do up here among the gums and the bottlebrush.

I feel I lectured. Not the intent.

Will press send before I hit delete, and continue after a stretch of the legs over to the dam.

Buen caminoooooooo . . .

A

178

What makes such an inexperienced kid like you SO WISE!

No lecture. Just rich insights. Might steal it for my homily this weekend.

Wish I had time to reply more fully now.

Gracias (now you've got me speaking Spanglish).

Shalom.

T

I'm back, as Arnie would say. Be afraid. Be very afraid.

The dam is worryingly low for this time of year. Lots of kangaroo prints around the edges. They will be getting thirsty if this early heat continues.

Meant to say that I loved attending the baptism, invited or no. Your words to the family gave me pause. I particularly liked your insistence that 'happiness' was not necessarily the best wish for a child, but rather we should wish for an embrace of the whole range of their emotions and character.

And I loved being 'backstage' with the robes and the 'props'–forgive the showbiz terminology! You know, girls were not allowed to be altar kids when I was little–perhaps if I'd had access to more of the ritual, then I might have stayed closer.

That said, I found it oddly confronting to see you in your priestly regalia–your costume. It's not that I'm unaware of your working life, or of your duties as a priest, but part of my irritation with almost all religions is the way the trappings help separate us into 'performer' and 'audience'.

I've always had mixed feelings about the paraphernalia of religion. It led me to a love of ritual as a child, and I suspect it may have taken me to the theatre, but when I returned as an adult seeking meaningful dialogue and interaction, I felt as though I'd matured, and the Church hadn't. I wanted communion–'the sharing or exchanging of intimate thoughts and feelings' as one dictionary defines it.

I think of my love of the word *'compañero'*–that bread-breaking is at the heart of the Mass, and how lovely it would be to be able to commune in such a way with those who share beliefs (and those who don't), as opposed to the structured, hierarchical 'staging' that is my experience of church-going.

I suppose I read space and costume in a particular way, given my years in the theatre, so the architecture of most altars and pulpits with their elevated areas for priests, and the elaborate expensive robes, and the monologue/rote nature of the service, all conspire to make me feel distanced.

But I digress. See what happens up here in the bush? Wow!

A flight of ducks just flew over—about a metre above my head. Immense burst of noise—an urgent flapping, not at all like the silent flight of the parrots when they swoop past. It's hectic here on the bird highway. Blue wrens, choughs, ibises on Ida's dam next door.

To your three-part recipe for relationship . . .

No, it's not gobbledegook, and I don't mind trying to label such progressions in order to mark or understand them, but that sequence doesn't describe my experience. I agree there is enchantment, if we are incredibly graced. I'm not mad on the words 'necessary disenchantment' to be honest. They imply something sour to me, but I take your point. I would probably choose to call that stage 'unveiling the ugly bits'! That process of revealing can break some bits of the fairytale, but they are usually replaced with a clear-eyed nonfiction narrative, which is intense and lasting. Learning to love 'in spite of' rather than 'because of' is how I think of it. The Camino never broke me without repairing me in better order, and that seems to me to be what happens with such relationships. Like the broken shell–light comes in through the cracks.

Finally, yes, hopefully there is consolidation, which may well be mature but which can also feel infinitely childlike. I'd probably prefer to call that phase, which is hopefully endless, 'deepening'.

I meant it when I said I felt I'd been tapping my foot, waiting for you to show up again in my life. That day at lunch I knew I knew you. I feel it quite deeply. I 'fall' frequently for people, love a little too easily perhaps, but THAT . . . no, that was not just the effortless freefall toward a shiny new playmate. There is something more, Tony, and I think maybe we suspected it when we encountered each other's words on a page for the first time–your article about the Camino hit home to me too, you know. It was verified for me when

I saw you and thought, 'There you are.' I recognised you as one of my tribe. I sat at lunch nibbling Chinese food while you greeted a string of folk and introduced me to them, but all the while I wanted to say, 'Where have you been all this time?'

So. There 'tis. A mystery–a favourite word for both of us.

I know what you mean about me taking on a Monsignor in public discourse or private correspondence, and yes, some of my personal village might think me worryingly close to either conversion or lunacy–but they don't pay my bills, and they know me well enough by now to understand that I will go where my heart leads–and it rarely leads me down blind alleys. The seeker is hijacked by 'what others think'–even if they are the near and dear. I could never have written the letter asking people to donate sins if I was worried what people would think of me.

No. That's not right.

I did worry what they'd think. But I did it anyway. What else could I do? Live life for others, or against an impulse that felt true. When my internal compass tells me a path north leads home, I can't walk south just because that road is more appealing to other people. I try to trust that what I'm doing is finding a way to incorporate as much as possible of the world into my small and ordinary existence.

Funny. If you were an Imam, friends might be equally anxious. Or perhaps not! That might be a more fashionable choice, just now. Or a Buddhist monk. Or a declared atheist. But fashion, as anyone can tell from looking at me, is not my shtick. My shtick is a walking stick, and you and I are two pilgrims walking together for a while. That's how I see it.

Yes, yes, wasn't it good to spend a couple of hours? Little it was, but also much. I've been reflecting on our conversation about my time in Sydney all those years ago. When I recall living there, I always picture jacarandas, the signature blossom of Sydney for me. How often I have flown in or out to that sea of mauve below, just as I did this last time. The street where I used to live was carpeted with them in November. They'd drift about me as I strolled from the Domain through the Botanic Gardens to the Opera House to see chums in a play, and I recall a glorious specimen over the road from a shared terrace house where I lived in Cathedral St in Woolloomooloo–about the time you were up the road being Dean of the actual Cathedral. Funny that I never went inside then, even for a peek.

A trifle embarrassing, when I think on it. Did I have so little curiosity?

But then, my cathedral doesn't have a man-made roof!

I must stop. Kangaroos are coming in to feed. The males are in spring fever and grunt at the females. Not at all fetching. The miracle is that they've forgotten I'm human, and graze away on the native grass oblivious to me. I could watch them for hours, but I must go and organise some human grazing.

Gracias, compañero.

This has been a good talk. I've enjoyed it.

A x

Ailsa,

Jacarandas, Woolloomooloo, the Domain . . .

You've conjured up a memory from a particular time, and a very particular incident. A particular woman.

Perhaps it can add a dimension to your image of me as a costumed magician on a high altar. Indulge me, if you will, by listening to a story.

Sunday's midday meal at St Mary's Cathedral was roast beef. Not to be missed. The rigours of a busy morning—celebrating masses, conducting a guided tour, dealing with dozens of people, and their questions—were all behind me. Cold beer and hot beef beckoned, perhaps even a glass of red.

And then the telephone rang—of course.

A ward sister at Sydney Hospital needed a priest. This was not an unusual request. Nor was the timing. A woman had died—'She was Catholic, Father'—and her son in Melbourne had asked if it was possible for a priest to anoint her, with the ancient ritual of farewell. Not disguising my interest in the beef with any great success, I collected the oils and headed for the door and the short walk to the hospital.

Sydney Hospital, part of the treasured heritage of this city, was conveniently no more than 500 metres away—three or four minutes walking time. It was November, the jacaranda was throwing its violet bells everywhere, a gentle, cooling nor'easter relieved a seriously sunny and warm day.

The woman was in the middle of a room, entirely devoid of furniture or other fittings. Walls and ceiling completely white. The body lying on a gurney covered neatly with a sheet. A stark and impeccable presence.

The nursing staff left me alone in the room.

I pulled back the sheet covering her. The body was that of a mature woman—how old? I found it hard to tell. Later, on examining the papers, I saw the record said 85. In its utter stillness the dead body concentrated my attention, but even more powerfully triggered my imagination and fired my curiosity.

Who was this woman?

How did she die?

Was she married? How many times? Was her son the only child? Were there grandchildren, perhaps? Siblings still living?

Who knew of her death?

Why was she alone?

The standard procedure in a moment like this is for the priest to follow an ancient ritual. Even in the situation when a person may have died some time before, the minister traces a small cross with the oils of anointing—first the forehead, then above each eye, each ear, then the mouth, The prayer 'with this holy anointing …' is recited. The ritual goes further. The heart, the hands and the feet are all anointed. The sacredness of the human body is simply and elegantly acknowledged. The unique story of each person's journey is celebrated. It is a moment of intense connection.

On this occasion, I was gripped in quite a special manner by the need to know more of this particular life. The story, her story, suddenly became of the utmost importance to me.

As a hospital chaplain in my early years of ministry, this enacting of the last rites of the Church became at times, sadly, almost routine. Other circumstances often distracted —a grieving family, nursing staff attending to the person, the details of hospital life. This day was different. I was challenging myself with the need to understand afresh just what I was doing. Here in this stark hospital room, what did my ministry really mean? What was the significance behind the simple action of anointing? It was almost as though I was performing the ritual for the first time.

It is not unusual, living as a priest, to feel challenged by people you love and admire to explain the ministry. Why do we do what we do? What is this strange magic that shapes our minds and contains our beliefs? Why all the vestments, pomp and ceremony?—as you wrote in your last mail. The insistence, sometimes quite passionate, to justify yourself, is rarely absent—spoken or unspoken. Or, at least, that is how it appears through my eyes.

This time I was asking the question, alone, without family present or hospital staff. This gave me the rare leisure and space to deeply reflect.

What was I doing with this woman whose heart had stopped beating two hours ago?

My curiosity prompted more questions.

Where was she, say, at the age of twelve? Happy? Playful? A loved member of a caring family? Good at school? Musically inclined?

What was her experience of human love? Was she married? Had she felt deep grief? What were her passions? Which were the questions that spurred her on? And what was I doing here with my oils and my crosses?

Suddenly a new sense of meaning flooded in on me.

I was saying farewell to another human being. I was acting on behalf of the community of people who had been touched by her life. In this clinically stark room I was charged with honouring the life of this woman at this moment of transition. I was given the sacred task of acknowledging who this woman had been, the journey that she had travelled, the love that she had hungered for and shared. Honouring that spirit which I believed was now experiencing the fullness of life.

For those whose lives end without such a farewell, I felt a great sense of loss.

As I left the room, to report to the ward sister, she placed a note in my hand with the telephone number of the grieving son. On telephoning him he revealed he was the son of an Australian digger. His mother and father conceived their only child on a short leave from the front in the early 1940s. The father returned and was killed soon afterwards. The son shared with me some of her story. It was a great gift— she came alive in my mind. Several years later, I stumbled on a photograph of his mother (she had been a well-known photographic model)—elegant, poised, strikingly beautiful. It wasn't the twelve-year-old I had searched for. She was eighteen.

Your questions help me to recall memories which are precious. Thanks. For the November jacarandas and the Sydney Domain.

Night night.

Ant

Hi Tony,

What a wonder to discover on waking. A gift. Thanks for taking the time to tell me such a tender story. It raises so many questions, the image of that woman alone on the gurney. I can't help wondering about her last hours, and whether a solitary departure was her choice.

I'm sure I've commented before that I'm more familiar with death than birth. Some see that as a lack, but I'm not so sure. Death can have wonder, too. Like you, I think the act of farewelling a body is sacred, and I'm sorry that so many of the traditional final rituals are now carried out by funeral directors. I found solace in brushing my mother's hair and rubbing moisturiser into her skin, just after she died. Little things, but somehow they helped me to understand that although she was gone, the love we shared was not. In those small but familiar actions, there was a promise to hold her memory, and an acknowledgement of her body's importance to me. That body brought me into the world, and it was profoundly important for me to care for it at the end. I remember being shocked at how small she was in death–this towering force, now shrunken by cancer–but also relieved to see her face free of pain-lines.

I'm grateful my last picture of her was not of struggle but of repose.

I had one experience of death that some might find unusual or even confronting, but it remains one of the most remarkable times of my life. A year after Mum died, I was part of a 'family' keeping a final vigil. It was at the request of my friend Greg, a theatre and television director with a killer smile and sparkly blue eyes. I thought Mum was too young to die at 57, but Greg didn't make 40. He was actually old compared to many others who died of HIV/AIDS back then. The wards of St Vincent's were like field hospitals in wartime–all those young men.

Greg had so much he still wanted to do–two lifetimes' worth of dreams and projects–but he exited with exemplary courage and style. He gathered ten of us around him for his final days, and we cared for him at home, sleeping in shifts so he was not alone, organising practicalities like food and cleaning, his bathing and medicine, and herding the waves of people who came to farewell him. I don't think he would have considered turning anyone away, though there were days when the rest of us wanted to slam the doors.

My abiding memories are of laughter, in spite of the way Greg was being ravaged, and the certainty that his time was running out before our eyes. We spent many hours sitting around him in the bathroom, because he had to remain perched on the toilet. I recall one night when he wept, heartbroken and humiliated because of the indignity of his 'bare-arsed' state. We were all pretty raw at that stage, and would have done anything to make him feel brighter, even for a moment. So what did we do? We removed our trousers and sat around him, equally bare-arsed, on the floor–like children in a playground. There was no shame or prurience; just a determination to do whatever it took to give him relief and to raise a smile.

We were a mixed group, brought together by our love of Greg. We all did our very best, every moment of each day. The instructions for his farewell–music, speeches, venue–were carried out to the letter. He was a director and had left nothing to chance. We gathered in one of the wharves down at Millers Point. The weather co-operated and at the last, doors opened onto the water of Sydney Harbour and bright white light flooded in as the volume pumped up on his favourite dance music.

Sometimes I've considered trying to write the story of those days but I can't. I only own a corner of it. There were nine others looking after him. There was his blood family—complicated, because of Greg being gay. There was his work and other friends—hundreds who loved him—and he was different with every person, as we all are. He was a library of stories, and I could never do justice to them. But we honoured him, I believe. Body and soul.

Greg would laugh at that. He didn't believe in souls or spirits or afterwards. He believed that when he closed his eyes, it all stopped. I think dying that way, clear-eyed and steadfast in the face of a void, is one of the bravest things I know. The promise of afterlife or reincarnation is something to hold. Greg had nothing. Only love.

Hmm.

I think I must stop writing about him now. It still can make me a bit wobbly, seventeen years later. Instead, let me tell you about my day so far, which has actually been a kind of birth.

I woke at 5 am, sat down at the dining table, and wrote the opening of my book. It has been eluding me for about two years. Now it is done!

Well, the first draft of the first pages is out, anyway. Let's not go overboard. My task for today was to return to that section, and I thought it would take all week, maybe all month, but I woke and it was there. Cooked. And I think it might really be the actual first chapter. All before 7.30!

I wanted to tell you, given our conversation in Sydney about the wee small hours being the best time to write.

Soft rain has started to fall. I was about to get up and walk, but perhaps I will stay beyond the easy, unearned idea, and see if there is another lurking. Also, I might just sit and let myself be still with the memories of best beloveds, and the smell of rain on parched ground. Endings and beginnings. It was ever thus, I guess.

May your day be full and productive and hap-hap-happy.

Ailsa

Good morning,

As I was reading those stories of the death of your mum, and your friend Greg, I couldn't help being caught up again in the power of being with people who are dying. There's something that cuts through all of the trivia that distracts us most of the time. It's extraordinary, isn't it? Beyond doubt, they are sacred moments.

Talking very personally, I find it hard to take my own mortality too seriously. You'd think that at 78 any sensible person would allow time for the subject. Perhaps I do, to some small extent—although now I think about it, even a brush with cancer over a decade ago failed to convince me to stop and reflect. I suppose it can be explained as no more than common or garden denial. But sometimes I speculate that it is about the nature of the work I do—baptising tiny babies one moment and celebrating a funeral the next; counselling terminally ill people and then reading to a class of eight-year-old kids; going from a bright-eyed couple preparing for marriage to an aged-care facility. It is often a kaleidoscope of life and death. Ironically, it leaves me feeling a bit bullet-proof... sometimes.

But to get to your writing...

I think the mistake you make is going to sleep. Allowing that explosive unconscious to start brewing up the Piper creative juices. That is what I mean by writing at 4 am. Magic happens.

Another thing that's patently obvious is what an unstoppable walker you must be. To make a comparison, if I had spent a couple of days away from home, I would be slumped in a chair falling to sleep over the cricket. This powerhouse friend of mine has hit the word processor and written half a book.

There is not the slightest jot of criticism in this—simply sheer admiration and not a little envy.

But let me tell you where I am.

Sunday was bursting with people and events. Read your material quite late and went to bed smiling. Rose early this morning and headed for my car to take me swimming and the battery was flat again. So I have been waiting for a mechanic to get me mobile—talk about disen-bloody-chantment. In half an hour I head for St Michael's Golf course right on the dramatic cliffs of the coast with surf hitting the rocks and me keeping my head rigid over my putts. Ask Peter—he would understand.

You're a firecracker of a woman—should put you on the Bridge on NYE.

Happy days.

Tony

Querido Antonio!

You know, it tickled me to think that you're approaching 80 and don't fret about mortality. I'm 25 years your junior, and I have felt the push of it in my back ever since I can remember. I am sure it is why I race at the world and have such greed for experiences and people. Most mornings, on waking, my first thought is 'Hooray, I'm still here.' I truly don't expect to be. Not sure why, but it fires me to move, to do, to meet, to greet, to gobble it up. I'm not at all skilled at sitting and reflecting on anything–but I suspect mortality is the one thing I do not need to give my attention to because I can't recall a time when it wasn't present with me as a spur. Quite a sharp one at that.

And on the subject of moving, I've just walked for four hours along forest trails, climbing so high that I can literally see for miles. Now I'm ensconced at the general store with coffee, and a corn and asparagus pie. This is our own one-bar *pueblo*, where one day, you must walk.

And no, no. I'm not unstoppable at all. Matter of fact, I relish the stops. My mind, which goes out dreaming when I walk, has to catch up with my body, to settle back into it. And you know, I can walk differently, more like a snail.

Anyway, as a reward for slogging, your email. Thank you. Hope the mechanic came and you are birdying or putting or jabbing or whatever you do.

I've had a swirl of ideas in the hills, sparked by a call asking me to perform a piece written by Michael McGirr. In it he makes reference to his wife, and that made me reflect what a loss he must have been to his parish and community when he left the priesthood to marry–and what a gain she might have been, had she been able to be the wife of a working priest.

A kookaburra just whipped past, like a dart through the garden. I'm grateful for our place up here among the peace of minimal digital interference. No television. Tiny internet grabs here at the store. Silence. Animals. So lucky.

Hope the golf is perfection.

Oh wait! I forgot. You've given up on perfection. Hope it was heaven!

A x

Good morning sunshine,

COINCIDENCE; COINCIDENCE; COINCIDENCE.

I am dogged.

Michael McGirr is one of my hero writers. I have even taken out some of his writing and tried to mimic that wonderful silken touch of his storytelling. An aeon ago I took his cousin (or his aunt or someone called McGirr) to a dance as a shiny young eighteen-year-old. I attended his ordination as a Jesuit. I have read everything he has written. I lust after his immense skill.

Your comment about McGirr and marriage leads to the controversial question of celibacy. Let me offer a few words. Not the last by any means. But a little toe into the water. Starting with my own story.

When I considered this life—as a young adolescent, and then later after working, studying and furiously socialising for six or so years—I think my choice for the priesthood and therefore a celibate life was based on people I had met, rather than some lofty, impersonal ideal.

Did I know what I was giving up? I guess not. Do we ever know what we are giving up when choosing one lifestyle over another? One of the great surprises for me on entering the seminary was not so much a matter of 'giving up'—I found a rich alternative life among stimulating companions. I'm sure that wasn't the experience of everyone, but for me, much of it was great fun and expanded my life enormously. Perhaps it was the age thing. I was a young man when I joined, and not an adolescent.

In choosing the life, I guess much of my trust was placed in celibate friends of mine, women and men, who seemed pretty sane—above average in their self-awareness and relationships, really, and with a good grasp of their sexual identity.

Going into the seminary at 22, the eight years ahead of me before taking the final commitment seemed a long way off. You eventually decide to enter the agreement not to marry about six or seven months before being ordained. I guess the years of seminary life gradually socialised me into that final choice.

Would I have been able to do better pastoral work if there was an opportunity to marry? Frankly I don't know. Would I have been a saner and better-balanced person? Don't know that either. If marriage meant I could write as well as Michael McGirr, I might give it serious consideration.

I don't put this story forward as an argument for obligatory celibacy—I think the future needs to be otherwise—but simply my story.

Tonight I attend Sandy's latest play, and we will meet afterwards. Your ears will burn.

Tony

PS This is written in haste. Still to reply appropriately to your lengthy weekend reflections.

Dear Tony,

Today is a plodding day. I'm writing, but it's like wading through Andalusian mud. This is a quick break to check work email, and I caught you instead. A treat.

Thanks for your reflections on the celibate life. You always seem pretty sane to me. Balanced, too. But then I'm the woman who wandered across a country carting sins— not a model for sanity, some would say.

I feel a bit uncomfortable asking you to speak about celibacy–I don't usually get into long raves with friends about how they negotiate their sexual lives. Certainly not with a parish priest!

Interestingly though, I have a couple of girlfriends who've always been single by choice, and they find it incredibly offensive that people feel they have the right to ask them how they cope without a man or regular sex, as though they are disabled, or not a fully realised person, because they've not had a long-term relationship. These are remarkable gifted women, with big hearts and creative lives. They are not 'old maids'–that ugly expression–or 'spinsters'. They are contributors of the highest order, and funny and full of life.

As an aside, on the subject of impertinent questions, people always feel mighty free to enquire after why I have not had children–as though it is some fatal flaw in my character. It was a choice Peter and I took for our own considered reasons, and I don't feel I'm in any way diminished by it. Just different roads taken. That said, I experience my sexual identity, and the expression of it, as an integral part of myself, and can't imagine making a choice for celibacy–particularly as a prerequisite for a career.

And therein lies the rub, for me–the word 'obligatory' with reference to celibacy. I think it's cruel to make it a condition of ministry–particularly when one considers someone like McGirr. If it sits easily for some people, that's great–it's a requirement of many spiritual traditions, I know–but I can see no humane reason to deny partnership and a family to those who would like to be able to live that life. Or, for that matter, to deny the community access to some wonderful ministers.

I guess that it's when I think about an edict like that, or about the refusal to allow women to be priests or to choose Popes, that I picture the Catholic Church as an overbearing father standing over a table of children who are quaking at the possibility that he will lose his temper. A bully who insists that it is 'my way or the highway'; someone who directs people to 'do as I say and not as I do', rather than, as the Gospel says, 'Do unto others.'

Sorry. Not directed at you. A blurt. Telling, I guess. That isn't at all how I see you, but I guess the truth is that it has been how I've seen the Church for many years.

Regardless, I'm grateful to you for sharing more of your story with me. I appreciate your candour and generosity, instead of resorting to a party line.

I will read the McGirr piece tomorrow night, and will do my best. Imagine him being such a hero of yours. Truth be told, I'm actually way more nervous about my other job, which is to introduce Helen Garner–MY hero. What do I say about the mountain?

OK, signing off now. It's wet here today. Maybe that explains the fuzziness.

A x

Ailsa, Ailsa, Ailsa,

Where to start?

A bullying father? It's a curious thing—a frequent image of the Church that comes to mind for me is a frail, aged mother grown old with her faults and limitations, her superstitions and rock-like prejudices, but one who has given life to me and whom I love with a passion.

If I am honest with you, reading your words hurts. Hurts, and renders me quite inadequate to answer you with truth and in words that would genuinely help you to appreciate the subtleties needing to be faced working in an institution like this.

Your anger is not new to me, of course. It simply puts into strong language the feelings of many, in this seriously fractured time, about the supposed blindness of those of us who identify with the Catholic Church.

Needless to say I am one such person.

It puzzles me how you can make the distinction between me, priest for a lifetime supporting the institution in all I do and all I say—not exempting myself from taking issue with many of the more controversial matters, of course, but nevertheless seen as a faithful cog in the big wheel—and this colossus called the Church. Like many others, you quickly separate the individual that you agree with and the big institution. It's not always logical to make this distinction.

To describe this gigantic network of good and bad, fragile and strong, arrogant and unsure, self-satisfied and battlers as a 'bullying father' is a little disconcerting, to say the least. One of the colourful gospel images is of a large net of odd fish pulled up on a beach. I prefer that. We're a pretty mixed lot, you know.

If I am passionately committed to one thing, it is to explain to you how challenging it is to wrestle with the ambiguities and tensions within the Church today, while at the same time holding on to integrity and attempting to be a genuine minister of the gospel.

It seems to me that each of us, whoever we are, has a fundamental choice to make: work with one's own individual resources to bring some sanity to a world broken in so many ways (and some have the genius to do this); or work within some larger group of people, say an institution, with all the weight in the saddle-bags that comes with that choice. Think of the Red Cross or Médecins Sans Frontières, for example. Such people choose to draw on the best traditions, accumulated wisdom, hard-won experience and human resources that such institutions offer.

In my experience, the struggle to work with the inevitable weight of an institution overwhelms some. For others the difficulties help them to grow. But for all it is a walk on a tightrope. I suppose the years spent chopping away at the coalface makes me guarded about hasty slogans or simplistic solutions. Or am I too fixed in my ideas? Dunno.

Talking about his own institution, a hero of mine, Jesuit priest Walter Burghardt, nailed it for me:

In the course of half a century (and more),
I have seen more Catholic corruption than most Catholics read of.
I have tasted it. I have been reasonably corrupt myself.
And yet I joy in this Church,
This living, throbbing, sinning people of God;
I love it with a crucifying passion.
Why?
For all the Catholic hate, I experience here a community of love.
For all the institutional idiocy, I find here a tradition of reason.
For all the individual repressions, I breathe here an air of freedom.
For all the fear of sex, I discover here the redemption of my body.
In an age so inhuman, I touch here the tears of compassion.
In a world so grim and humourless, I share here rich joy and earthly laughter.

In the midst of death, I hear here an incomparable stress on life.

For all the apparent absence of God, I sense here the presence of Christ.

Haven't addressed your issues of the significant role of women, and I'm sure a dozen other issues that could be discussed, such as the horror of sexual abuse. But enough already.

May the conversation continue.

Tony

My dear Tony,

Firstly, an apology. I'm so sorry. Hurt was the last thing I wanted to give. I'm appalled that my hastily typed words caused pain. They were not written in anger, as you suggest. Quite the reverse. They were thrown down in a stream-of-consciousness rave, without any thought that they were contentious or personal for you. Stupid. Careless.

Reading them now, I can see how you must have felt them to be an attack, particularly when you write that you find it hard to understand how I can make a distinction between you and the Church.

I do make a distinction, I guess. I see you as my friend–person and not priest. Naïve, perhaps, but I've always tried to do that in my relationships–it's why I have many friends with opposing political viewpoints–but that does not give me permission to forget that you are a priest, or to be careless of that fact.

I admire the work you do, Tony–the good counsel, the open door, the humour, the perpetual readiness to serve and the empathy of your ministry; your big heart, shoulders and ears. And of course, they are the result of the experience and training of your vocation as much as your character.

Truth is, I've not had cause to name my attitudes on any of these subjects for years, because the Church no longer figures in my daily life. It was a part of my past. And when I say 'the Church', I should explain that I mean all organised religions. Yes, I grew up Catholic, but stopped having regular contact with churches when the choice was mine to make.

Why?

Well, that's almost as complicated as asking why you're a priest. But here goes . . .

My parents divorced back in the early 1960s, when I was a fair-haired tot who would not have understood that love can change. I just knew that something broke. The word 'divorce' was a whisper that followed my parents across the playground, but I didn't immediately connect it to Mum's absence from tuckshop duty.

By the time I was Head Girl (yes, afraid so) at a Catholic ladies' college, I was more aware of the subtleties of double standards. Schooled to admire the nuns who ran a thriving business—our school—without men, I also accepted I would never see one of those formidable females celebrating the Mass. Told that my teenage body was a temple, I also came to see it as a site of temptation.

Perhaps it was this history of confused standards and messages that made me drift away, because I was always searching for meaning. I wanted signs and sacredness, but I didn't want them at a cost to my sense of worth. That was fragile enough as a woman trying to make a way through the world on an equal footing with men.

I looked outside Catholicism to other religions and spiritual disciplines, but frankly, most of them had women as vassals or foot-soldiers, and I, daughter of a woman who'd encouraged me to believe I was equal to any bloke, found that disappointing at best, infuriating at worst.

Oddly enough, the way I see it, some atheists aren't a whole lot better on that score either! I've often found Mr Dawkins to be a strident, testosterone-heavy voice of certainty, too.

Ironically, given my opinionated swipe at the Catholic Church, the thing I find most difficult about many atheists and believers is their posture of certainty. Let me say here that I most definitely do not see that in you. Our friendship has taught me that you strive to see more than 50 shades of grey nuance.

I bear no anger to those who live peaceably within any religion–Buddhism, Islam or Zoroastrian. Really I don't, Tony. I say again–I envy them, sometimes. I remain grateful for the Catholic teachings I received, and am awed by much of the work done by contemporary Catholics, particularly for refugees. I mourn for Catholics who are confronting the abuse saga, and I am proud to call you my friend–very proud!-not least because I think your work is vital and inspiring.

But I've also spent years feeling that my existence was, in some never-quite-defined way, secondary to my male counterparts, and that was exacerbated by the Church's hierarchies. I've also had to battle the sense that my divorced mother was 'fallen'-that there was shame attached to that love-filled dynamo.

Now I realise I've written you a long letter about the institution of the Church, and not about you. Apologies again. Interestingly, I see that word 'institution' as one of the big differences between us. As you said, you work inside one, and I work outside. Not always by choice, and of course, from time to time I am inside walls, but essentially I'm not part of any organisation.

Occasionally a gatekeeper invites me to enter, but mostly I'm looking in through a grille. I accept that is a narrow view, but I do observe the effects of organisations out in the world, and many of them are not welcoming to me as a woman-be they corporate, government or religious.

We've got a female prime minister and I can't say I feel thrilled about the way she is being treated. Whether she is doing anything different to her male counterparts is not really the point for me—it is just a relief that we know it is now possible for an Australian woman to hold that office. I suspect there are female corporate titans who are just as tough as any bloke—but let's have more. Until we are normalised, we will always be the second sex.

Again—apologies for hurt. I hope you know that would never be my intention. I value our friendship too highly. It was thoughtlessness and haste. I should have written by hand. Remember the lessons of the snail, Ailsa.

I too hope the conversation can continue.

Ailsa

PS Love the Burghardt, though I have a suspicion that, with the exception of the last line, it could be said by a passionate insider from many communities or institutions. You could even try substituting the word 'family' for 'Catholic Church' and see what I mean.

By the way, I prefer the fish in the net image to your picture of the Church as a little old lady. And I agree, it is better than my bully.

Ailsa,

I find it hard to come up with any killer argument to convince you of where I am coming from in answer to your comments about women and religion in a brief email.

For now, I suppose a key phrase is 'the way I see it'. I think I subscribe to the view that we don't see things as THEY are. We see them as WE are. That our past experiences colour how we receive information—particularly, may I say, experiences of hurt or other distress. I quite happily concede that my perspective is that of a male who has worked for over 50 years ploughing this field—yes, a perspective coloured by my date of birth, the unusual workplace I occupy, the eccentric people I mix with (not exempting present company, I assure you), the conversations I engage in, the material I read, my particular sense of humour—all of which has me see the world the way I see it.

To be aware of one's limited perspective does not entirely free one from being blind to certain issues, of course, but I fondly believe it helps.

Ant

Hello again Ant,

We do argue from different perspectives, and not just gender and age.

But I have learned from this exchange, as I do with so many of our emails. From my side of our boundary fence, let me say that I'm grateful for your preparedness to find time to explain your positions. Would that our leaders–political and religious–might take a leaf from your book.

Ailsa

Ailsa,

A final rumination!

I'm sure you'll enjoy a story I heard once about male prejudice, although I fear I am simply loading your guns. It comes from the 19th century history of the suffragette movement. The husband of one activist, on hearing that women were to be given the vote, and knowing that his world was falling apart, was heard to say: 'Where are we going to draw the line?'

To which his wife replied:

'Who gave you the pencil?'

Happy days.

Ant

PS And I promise you I didn't even pick up a pencil.

SUMMER

Antonio!

Just went walking to clear the head after our exchanges, and saw an echidna swimming. He was blowing bubbles! Really. I thought of you, swimmer.

And when he heaved himself from the water, he got right on with his job. I was fascinated by his commitment to task. Find ants. Find ants. Find ants.

Well, I have found an Ant, too. And he makes me laugh, even when part of me feels murderous about his views. Loved the suffragette story. Thanks. I will be holding my pencils very close.

Must end here, but I suspect that we have located the 'labels' that we must be mindful of–cleric and feminist.

Back to the big smoke I go, carrying the image of a chortling echidna. Maybe that will stave off my nerves about the McGirr/Garner event.

Buen caminooooo!

A

Dear Ailsa,

Like the image of an echidna—lots of spikes, likes to burrow, loves to swim. Me to a tee!

By the way, I meant to tell you that I saw Sandy last night in her play. Loved it. Four talented young actors and the towering figure of Sandy. Her timing is impeccable. Interesting and hugely entertaining.

Travel safely.

Tony

Dear Tony,

I'm nursing a mighty non-alcohol-related adrenaline hangover.

I want so much to describe last night to you, but it was all love and fellow-feeling. That experience doesn't just slide onto the page, sadly. Some moments . . .

When Helen Garner arrived, she reached across to say hello, and I remember thinking, 'This is my great hero squeezing my hand.'

I read Mr McGirr and felt a wash of gratitude for my years in the theatre, which gave me the skills to honour other people's words. I heard remarkable tales of people's relationship to story. I read my intro and managed not to cry or shake.

Then Helen read. She spoke about the physical act of writing, of pens and backaches and ink-stains and things solid and real and, as always, true.

Bruno, who makes these nights happen, spoke of his father, a Sicilian gardener who never really 'got' what Bruno did as a teacher. Bruno says that now, ironically, he sees himself as a gardener, just like his dad. Last night he harvested.

You will be happy to know that you were present, Antonio! A lady told me her husband was at our conversation, and that he lies in bed every night with my book, chortling away or sighing at passages of my journey. She said her husband loved our talk, and she watched it on video afterwards. She wished she'd been able to come, not least because–'That Tony Doherty is rather sexy!'

Now I have to tell you I was taken aback at this full and frank admission, but she kept on glowing over you. I'm not sure it's wise to report her comments. But she was a fan of yours, and, as you can see, last night spread its arms wide, extending them to Rose Bay.

It's going to be thirty-eight degrees down here today. I think you have something similar. I have two meetings this morning, and then will be locked away with the computer, sweating my way through a list that is stopping me from getting back to the book.

And tomorrow . . .

My friend Louise, a boundless spirit, will drive me up to our shack in her car (I do love to be a passenger), and we will walk and walk for three days. And talk. She has been away for two months, meditating and restoring, and I've ached for her like a missing limb. We've been down every tunnel imaginable in our friendship–enchantment and consolidation and way beyond. We've faced dragons in each other, and helped to slay them. I love her fiercely and in a way that can only exist when you have, yes, deepened. And I have three days of her.

On Sunday she will return to town and my younger sister, Amanda, will come up to spend Sunday night. We will walk on Monday morning.

A feast. Can't believe I deserve it, but I'll take it and be glad.

I hope you may have equal joy in your days, Antonio. I hope you slept long and deep. I seem to be in a cycle of brief sleep just now, but there's so much waking loveliness, why miss it? Yesterday, on the train into the city, I thought I might cry because I was so happy for no reason—and then suddenly I was heartbroken for my mother and the many friends who have died and not known third or fourth or fifth decades here on the planet, heart beating and sun shining and love overflowing.

I must stop. I've written four letters so far, and now I'd better go and tidy the house and get ready to appear sane at my meetings.

I hope that life/work is fulfilling for you, and that the harbour shimmers at its most sparkly. I hope you are peaceful and productive. And that you are cool! Physically, I mean. We know you are cool in every other way. That lady last night would have nothing less!

Hasta pronto.

Ailsa

Ailsa,

Your first words about the hangover left me concerned that something went wrong—like forgetting Helen Garner's name or making highly ambiguous mistakes in reading the McGirr material. Sheer relief to find that the exact opposite was the case. A night pressed down, shaken together and flowing over. The wonder and delight of artists tasting the juices of life and conversation. Your description lifted my spirits.

I hate this copycat behaviour of mine—but I have a secret literary relationship with H. Garner. A national treasure and you are not the only puppy dog in love with her.

Three days of walking with Louise sounds dreamy. You have an extraordinary capacity, if I may be so bold to say, to live your life to the full—you inspire me. Makes my daily 30-minute plunge into the harbour scarcely able to be remarked upon.

Thanks for the precious opportunity of hearing the detail of last night. You're a most generous friend.

Happy days.

Tony

PS Hope you got the address of the fan who considered me (can I say the word without blush?) 'sexy'. Tell her the fan club meetings are held in a phone box in Old South Head Rd on months that have 32 days in them.

But please don't think I am anything but tickled pink.

T–

I had to laugh just now. I read your comment about me living life to the full just after I had taken a breather on the couch to eat a salad and do a Sudoku (addict!). Before I'd finished either, I told myself to get up and get to the computer because I was wasting time.

My challenge is in sitting still and NOT doing. It's a problem. Because I know deep in my bones that all this wonder can be snatched away at any second, I feel compelled to gobble it up. I've had too many best beloveds leave without warning with lives unlived, so I know it can happen, and I rush at it all. But sitting still is a grace, and I'm trying to learn more of it. Louise is a Vipassana practitioner and can sit for hours. I admire it so. I think it was Blaise Pascal who wrote that all the evil in the world can be traced to our inability to sit still in a room. If that is true, I am a wicked perpetrator of said sin. I am still trying just to slow down!

Here's a lovely thing. In the time it has taken me to write a blog post and this email, a new baby came into the world—she will bear the name of my grandmother Elsie—and one of my favourite 'godsons' has come through surgery and is sitting in hospital eating sushi. Louise writes that she has stewed rhubarb as a treat for tomorrow. My little sis, Amanda, writes that she went to the Immigration

Museum and looked up Piper in one of the record books. There she found a history of our mob. One of them was a Thomas Piper, who became a Christian pastor. It was said of him that he was 'a fervent preacher often blending keen logic and holy passion with remarkable effect.' I wonder if I would have liked him. Anyway, what a swag of email. I'm almost afraid to ask what is happening outside my mailbox!

Alright, pilgrim. That's all the break I've earned. Trust you're not as hot up there as we are in Melbourne, but equally delighted by the way the world turns.

A x

Ailsa,

I smile every time you address me as pilgrim. Has the ring of a John Wayne movie about it!

7 am.

Just come still dripping from the harbour, every cell and artery wide awake. Just as well, because one of my swimming mates raised the ever-controversial topic of celibacy as

I emerged from the water. Sometimes I have a private bet with myself when going to dinner with friends, about the amount of time it will take before it comes up in conversation. But at my favourite beach ...!

Anyway, I'm going to risk another small earthquake from you and open it up again. In the last few years, the link between celibacy and the general disgust about paedophilia has taken top billing. Understandable, of course. The most widespread opinion claims that sexual abuse of children by celibate priests is easy to fathom. Eliminate the obligatory celibacy and you eliminate the abuse. QED.

Well ... I'm not so sure. I suppose I would say that, wouldn't I? But I have an aversion to easy targets, an even greater aversion to over-simple solutions.

In this post-Freudian, post-modern, wonderfully enlightened world, sometimes I get the impression that some think they know more about the mystery of human sexuality than in fact they do. Even the research into the general causes of paedophilia is pretty thin. The issue of priests abusing children, I suspect, has many causes: and I believe that the hard work has yet to be done to identify and eradicate these causes.

This is not to argue that an obligatory celibate lifestyle

undertaken as a condition for ministry is not to be seriously examined—simply that the matter may be far more complex than much of the debate would admit.

But let's go back to where all this began—Michael McGirr. His writing has that wonderful lightness—not unlike your own may I say without flattering—touching the mysteries which make up our life while happily avoiding the frozen religious language that only serves to wash off us. His writing lands on the page as lightly as a butterfly with sore feet.

A bit lyrical I know. But remember I've been splashing in Sydney Harbour.

Must go.

So let's go pil ... grum!!!

Tony

Dear Tony,

Can't answer this fully as I'm up country with Louise, fed and watered in our oft-practised kitchen dance, and elated at having time with her; but I read your comments about the link between celibacy and paedophilia with interest. I agree that the causes of abuse are likely to be way more varied and complicated than much of the commentariat would have it. I remember some years back when the gay community were having to defend themselves daily from zealots who insisted there was a direct link between homosexuality and paedophilia. My blood boiled, as I thought of my gay friends who are exemplary parents, and others who've fostered children for years.

We've got so accustomed to being given a quick sound-bite answer to things. If it were as easy as that, wouldn't life be grand? And how to explain that the majority of sexual abuse happens in the home, and by heterosexuals?

I don't know. Don't understand. I can't face it. I guess all I'd add is that in terms of the priests who prey on children, it's about abuse of power and trust as much as anything else. But then isn't all abuse about that?

Enough, now. Up here among the gum trees, just for today, I would like to free my mind from darker thoughts. I want to give my head a chance to roam. Earlier, I sat down to write my last blog post thinking I knew what it would be, only to find myself far, far away, writing about something I didn't know. I like it when I can give my thoughts some time to wander.

As an aside, does that ever happen to you with sermons? Do you always know in advance where a reflection will end?

Sorry I'm rushing. I want to offer thoughts that are formed and considered. Talk would be good. A couple of armchairs on either side of a coffee table. Time . . .

Good night. Can't believe I was in Sydney a week ago. It seems like three lifetimes.

Ailsa

Ailsa,

Just arrived back from the wedding of the youngest daughter of a lifelong friend of mine—whom I buried a couple of years ago—on their property ten kilometres outside Bega. Gorgeous rolling hills, technicolour green, dotted with homesteads. The ceremony was under an ancient elm tree on the side of a hill. At the critical moment of sharing vows we were hit with a violent wind sweeping up the valley—the spirit was alive and well (it was quickly interpreted by the romantics among us as the enthusiastic sign of approval from the bride's late father).

As is not unusual in the bush, the wedding party went until the early hours—vigorous and highly charged 30-somethings dragging my rather inflexible frame on to the dance floor. My clunky attempts to engage in the exhilarating gyrations of my new young friends were covered in deep embarrassment. Vain protests that 'I am more a walker than a dancer' were drowned in the electronic din. Thank God for good wine. Happily I have lived to tell the story—as they say 'never underestimate a survivor'.

Talking writing ...

I may not be ready to write about the abuse disaster but I have invited interested people in the parish to come together next Tuesday to discuss/express their anger/vent their frustration and bewilderment, and decide what we are going to do about it. Will be interesting to see who turns up and what transpires. Hold the presses.

You asked me about sermons.

Not sure where to start, but I sometimes have a pathological unease about religious language. Another deep concern I have is about anything that approaches cliché. The trouble is that if I have heard some expression only once or twice, it goes straight into the cliché file. That leads to some amusing situations. Because I celebrate Mass twice on Sunday mornings, I have a distinct revulsion of giving the same homily again at the third mass at night. My low boredom threshold stands exposed. Take note!

You said something about starting your blog in one direction and the writing taking off on some entirely new angle as you write. Well sunshine, that's me to a tee. I prepare quite assiduously, but if something else takes my notice … off I go. The language sensitivity thing, however, is deeply ingrained—God language, particularly. I wonder what your revered Scottish ancestor man of the cloth would make of my touchiness.

To be a little clearer about what I mean by 'God language'—it's the stuff that we hear repeatedly from church pulpits, often abstract, often from the Greek tradition of the Creeds. I heard a phrase that has always stuck in my mind as a warning—'Words falling from pulpits like frozen birds from a winter sky.' Of course, the Greek analytic language is part of the Christian package, but it is always instructive to me that Jesus talked mostly in story language, almost never in formulas.

Thinking of winter skies reminds me of when, as a boy of ten and still in short pants, I was invited to tour an observatory equipped with a powerful telescope. The director of the observatory, a gentle old Jesuit astronomer, was attempting to fire young minds with the wonders of the universe. Each boy eagerly took his turn to look through the lens. For some reason, when my turn came, I failed to focus on anything before being pushed along by the next in the queue impatient to have a look. Always have been a little slow to see things. Disappointed, but now alone outside the observatory, the telescope experience was not completely wasted. Looking up at the night sky, the stars of the Milky Way leapt out at me, splashed like a handful of diamonds carelessly strewn over velvet cloth. I had scarcely noticed it before. I was hypnotised by its vast magnificence. A moment of genuine 'awe'. It may have been my first experience of the depth of that word.

From my very centre, questions arose. Who am I? How did I come to be here? How far are those stars away from us?

What were the names of those other stars and planets? There has been an explosion of information about the universe, of course, since those days—the first satellites were launched; there was the excitement of the moon landing; photos appeared of Planet Earth in a sea of darkness. We have all learned about a universe that is expanding, about something called 'the big bang', about the distance light travels from the nearest star. More information—strangely, never matched by that first experience of awe. The boy never grew out of the questions: Who am I? How did I come to be here? But now there were other questions. Where can we find meaning in this amazing universe? Where is 'God' in all of this? Keenly he felt the need of that ancient Jesuit priest/astronomer to help answer the questions. How could the old Jesuit balance the intricate and sophisticated science of astronomy with the stories of his biblical faith? How could he celebrate the mystery of the Eucharist each morning and then spend much of his night peering into the mystery of the unfolding universe? Twelve years after that observatory visit, I would follow my gentle teacher along the long path he had already walked—to commence studying to be a priest.

Let me say something about the enthusiasm I had with the study of scripture. Reading the bible is a puzzle. We talk about it—often with entirely false confidence—quote from it, swear on it, prop it on our bookshelves, fight over its meaning, write our family genealogy in its flyleaf. Few really understand it. Not a single book, the bible is a collection of books written for different purposes, but written by people, dare I say it, rather like ourselves, wrestling with the questions that take us to the centre of our being human: What does love mean? What is this brief life of ours about? Why do some people die young? How can we live in justice and peace? The language of their stories is often unfamiliar—remember they were written as long as 3000 years ago, by people who were as nomadic as the early Indigenous people of our own continent.

The Jewish tradition very sensibly refrains from naming God. The modesty contained in this prohibition always seemed eminently sensible to me. A writer friend of mine (see—I have writer mates, too!) claims that to speak appropriately about God is not only difficult but can be dangerous. Not only ministers of religion, but journalists, politicians, taxi drivers, even teachers of religion, throw the word around with abandon without ever having any real idea what they are talking about. 'It is a tragedy of modern western culture,' he claims, 'to have fallen victim to the illusion that it is perfectly easy to talk about God.'

The seminary taught me many things. One of the most important was: to know what you know, to know what you don't know, and to be able to tell the difference. To me the mark of an honest preacher is to hold tightly to that principle.

Ironically, while people today frequently move away from the notion of a biblical God, there seems to be no diminishment in the hunger for a spirituality that is able to nourish the questions we ask ourselves. Like the word 'God', the word 'spirituality' is far from easy to define. I learned recently that the word soul (or spirit) originally meant 'coming from or belonging to the sea'. There is something about the endless sky and the restless sea that keeps us awake to the unique human experience we share, wrapped in the arms of a gentle gracious mystery. The questions of the boy looking up into the night sky all those years ago are not unfamiliar to any of us.

Excuse the length of this mail—you must be dropping off to sleep reading it. As the drunk said in the police station—'I had the right to remain silent, but I didn't have the ability.'

Antonio

Hi Ant,

I'm so glad you didn't remain silent, dear drunk! What an astonishing letter. I am a poor creature with no time today, and can only bow in humility at that offering before I race out into the too, too rushed morning. So sorry. But I will read and re-read it through the day. One of the pleasures of digital correspondence.

In passing, though, I wonder if I could go a day without using the word God. We are so casual with it, as you say . . .

God knows.

OMG.

Good God.

God help us.

God! (Expletive, pleasure, awe . . . whatever)

And that is just the habitual, unconscious tics we have.

The Jewish tradition might be very sensible. I am going to try to monitor myself with this. Perhaps I should be saying 'Oh my stars' or 'Good eucalypt' or 'Sun help us'. After all, that worked for the ancient Greeks with Neptune and Artemis and Zeus.

You write of 'the Greek tradition of the Creeds', and of 'words falling from pulpits like frozen birds', and my ears prick up—not just at that lovely metaphor, either.

Can you open up for me what you meant by 'Greek analytic language'? I thought Hebrew was the basis of most of the Christian 'package'.

Sorry to take you to Theology 101, but I'm curious. And sorry to meet such a letter with a request for another. I am Oliver Twist—'More, please.'

Only when and if you can . . .

Deep gratitude for unearned grace.

Ailsa

Ailsa,

What I meant by that heavyweight Hebrew/Greek comment is that there are two different influences in the history of Christianity—sometimes it makes things a little clearer for me, at least, to keep them in mind.

One is the Hebrew way of thinking. The other is the Greek—more abstract, more analytic. They are quite different. The Jewish tradition is held together, by and large, by stories. Think of the creation account, Adam and Eve and all that. Jesus was a Jewish storyteller. Explaining his vision for a more human world, he used story after story. This was a classic Hebrew way of communicating.

But the Christian movement began to spread throughout a Mediterranean world and adapt to its new culture, often Greek-speaking and Greek-thinking. St Paul's letters are a good example. There are few stories in Paul, and more analysis, expressed more often than not in abstract language.

Later, when the Roman Emperor Constantine wanted to unify the empire, and heal the hotly debated divisions in the Church, a Council was called. Amidst all the argy-bargy and debate, a statement of basic beliefs was formulated—the Nicean Creed was born. It was expressed in the most abstract of language, taken from that very analytic Greek tradition. Now, each Sunday, we recite a version of that Creed faithfully, but dare I say most still struggle to understand its meaning fully. Sometimes I find myself asking, 'why couldn't they have just left us a story?'

In my funny perspective on things, I think there is a good example of these two ways of thinking that happens in libraries. Placing books into strict categories—crime, travel, spirituality—is very Greek. Logical, working from clear distinctions etc. But the books themselves are frequently stories—far harder to categorise. Think of your book. It could easily have been filed or displayed under the categories of memoir, travel, spirituality or even extreme sport!

But to return to my high-minded explanation, the fact that our Christian tradition borrows from many sources can only be a plus, don't you think?

But enough with the God language. Hope it helped.

Tony

My dear Tony,

Let's cop a little God talk on our chins! I can cope, after the last 30 minutes. A neighbour has just finished telling me of her son's abuse by the parish priest around the corner from us, one of the most serious of all the offenders on record. Terrible. Beyond depraved.

I'm home alone tonight–Peter is up country–rain beating down outside, and I can't lift myself off the chair. After talking to that neighbour, I opened my computer and read a letter from a friend in the army telling me of the abuse suffered by wives at the hands of some of the returning Vietnam vets who had been 'serviced' by girls trained as prostitutes. The men came home and demanded similar service from their wives. What could these 'bland, Anglo women' do to compete? How had the Vietnamese girls been taught their 'tricks'? What were the soldiers really wanting?

Heartbreaking.

I had an utterly beautiful day, but this half hour has taken all wind from sails.

I'm grateful for your missive. It brings light. Which is not to say that is all I expect from you. Sorry. Of course not that. Be however you are. At any time.

Just meant . . .

Thanks for the 'talk'. I can't seem to write much of anything just now in reply. I will respond properly, hopefully in the bright new early morning. Which it will be.

I hope you have a warm still night up there in Sydney. Melbourne is cold and the house is rocking with wind. Turbulence.

A x

Ailsa,

Dawn breaking over Sydney Harbour. Peaceful and already warm. Just heading for the water and read your mail and what a horrible night you were having. There is a guy named Richard Holloway (wonderful, searching, honest pilgrim of life) who wrote a strange but comforting book *Between the Monster and the Saint*, which he concludes with the words:

It is a harsh world, indescribably cruel.
It is a gentle world, unbelievably beautiful.

It is a world that can make us bitter, hateful, rabid, destroyers of joy.
It is a world that can draw forth tenderness from us, as we lean towards one another over broken gates.
It is a world of monsters and saints, a mutilated world, but it is the only one we have been given.
We should let it shock us not into hatred or anxiety, but into unconditional love.

When you told me the story of the soldiers returning from the Vietnam War and abusing their wives—I thought of the Holloway statement. In wartime, no soldier goes unwounded, but they didn't say that to my father coming out of France in 1918. Or friends of mine who had returned from Kokoda in 1945. Today, thank God, there is more awareness of this abuse.

In short, war abuses soldiers. Soldiers often abuse women. Where does such abuse cease? We don't know. The cycle of violence continues.

Holloway unflinchingly faces the 'indescribable cruelty' that exists, yet offers the alternative. Our lives are played out between the monster and the saint, and each of them exists within our own skin.

Love that line about broken gates.

Sent with a big hug.

Tony

Dear Tony,

Holloway's words resonated with me very deeply, though I'm not sure I can be quite as clear-eyed as him about the world. Part of me is a romantic who wants to buy into the idea that the 'world' is pure and untarnished, and that it is we humans who make the mess. But that makes me separate from the world, and that is nonsense. The easy cop-out, perhaps. I'm not quite as unflinching as Holloway yet, but I'm trying.

Thank you. I am rolling his words around in my mind. And I guess if I'm honest I feel like I am the broken thing, rather than the gate.

I've been wrestling with myself about this email. I want to sit down and write you a proper letter, slowed down to body-speed, not tapped out at this ridiculous keyboard-pace that creates errors and skims the surface. But I also want the immediacy of conversation. The to and fro. So I've given in and come here to my drug of choice, the computer. But I will do the other thing, too. I will take paper and pen and slow down, later today, when this tumult has settled. Perhaps after walking.

This shouldn't surprise me, but it does. Always, when I have had an overload of joy or of sorrow, there has to come a balancing. The world sends it. It's as sure as night following day, and yet I'm tripped up and I fall. Once, earlier this year, I actually fell physically, so hard did the wisdom need to slap me. But I am getting something of the message. Slowing down is the insistent theme. Slow every-thing. Attend more closely. Don't just smell the roses, but sit with them, maybe until they have withered. Stay.

So hard. It has always been the hardest thing for me. Stay.

Anyway, I'm going to try to type more slowly, and to take things chronologically . . .

On Saturday, while you were marrying your friend's daughter, I hit the hills with Louise. Our jaws had as good a workout as our legs, while you were feeling the wind of a father's love sweep up the valley and swirl around a bride. I love that image. I love to picture you, looking into the eyes of your old friend in his daughter's face, and somehow holding all those forces. No wonder you danced!

We danced across hills, too, and I talked to Louise about slowing down, and she talked about sitting still, as we whirled. I'm getting out of chronology here, but I sourced a Richard Holloway radio conversation, after reading the darkly hopeful quote you sent me. In that lilting brogue, he talked of falling in love with another student, as a young man. A male student. Something about the ease with which he spoke of it made me relieved. I've always said I can fall in love with anyone–male or female, young or old, straight or gay–and people ask me to pin that down. Oh, are you bisexual?

'Were we talking about sex?' I want to shout back at them.

Because, and don't take this the wrong way, Tony– sometimes I fall in love a dozen times a day. The grumpy guy who sells me flowers. The girl on the train with the dreadlocks and the tattoo of a bluebird. The old lady practising tai-chi despite her crooked back. The spotty-faced schoolboys in a cluster at the station. The pasty-faced Goth playing football with his little fair-haired sister. The bloke who talks gibberish at me non-stop all the way down Swanston Street. The Italian *nonna* walking her arthritic chihuahua. The men on the trams, pressed and tied and suited and grey, looking away, into the distance. The old man who smells faintly of mustiness and urine, shuffling his walking frame to get the morning paper. The effort. The work it takes to keep going, to stay in life, in love, while the heart beats on.

Sometimes I am swept away by a kind of happiness that comes from just being in the world. Seeing a hint of shimmer in everyone. I know that sounds Pollyanna-ish, but it isn't how it feels. It just feels like I'm seeing them–and maybe wishing for them, though the wish is unspecified. I hesitate to say something as sweeping and broad as 'happiness'. There is a definition of love that says it is wanting the best for someone else. Well, in those moments, maybe that is what I'm doing, without knowing it. Wishing.

Loving. Whatever. I do it rather a lot, and I don't know why it should feel embarrassing to own up to it, but sometimes it does. As though I am indiscriminate or, God help us, soft. Sentimental.

Maybe I am, but I wouldn't trade those moments for all the rational cool on the planet—and I suspect those times, and when I'm walking, are as close to holiness as I get.

Which brings me back to Louise! I love her with a kind of ardour born of immediate knowing, followed by breaking of and by each other, followed by calm, followed by recognition—and we both know it, speak of it, and understand it for what it is. A gift.

And so we walked and talked, of people and places and dreams. You were with us some of the time. Maybe a wind gust came south and made me think of you. And I was glad.

At day's end we returned to the house and made dinner to share with Peter, who had arrived in his old silver sedan. It was great to feel the leg and conversational muscles twitching then dissolving—even as yours would have been contracting and prancing around the dance floor.

Sunday brought more gifts. We took the high road to the general store where once per month a group of Spanish speakers meet for coffee and talk. Lou sat and watched me natter in *Español*, Peter came to pick us up, and we three lunched together, admiring the wood he had cut and the fires that were burning in prep for the summer season. Scary here. The grass is long and drying out fast. They're predicting another horror of heat, and so circles of safety are being cut before fire restrictions begin on Monday.

Louise left. I had to change sheets and prep the spare room, because my little sister Amanda was arriving–which she did, bringing her gentle maturity and quizzical smile. She is smart, considered and reserved, and the eighteen years between us is present but never an obstacle. She allows, does Amanda. So we sat by one of Peter's fires in the field, sipped red, and caught up. And later that night, I stood on the deck in the pitch dark with Peter, looking up at the bazillion stars in the blackness. He does that every night before he turns in. It's his ritual. Your old Jesuit would approve.

Yesterday, Amanda and I repeated the high hill walk to the store and then had lunch in their kitchen garden with Peter, the walker's friend. Then, at Amanda's suggestion (she understands the need for slow!), she and I had half an hour of reading time before cleaning up and heading into Melbourne. En route, we stopped for Amanda to take some photos at a weird place at the end of the Tullamarine runway where plane-watchers sit in a car park to look at the underbellies of aircraft.

I was exhausted when I got home. Happy exhausted.

There was an unusually large pile of mail waiting, but what grabbed my attention was two packages. My father's distinctive handwriting adorned one, and, with a shock, I realised the other was from Brett, the older of my two brothers. I don't know why, but it made me crack that I didn't recognise his handwriting. I felt like I had missed something vital. He's a big Aussie bear of a bloke, this brother, and yet his letters are classically shaped and clear. They are like his mind—no fancy curlicues, measured, evenly spaced. I can't say why it made me so vulnerable. We communicate by phone and email, but handwriting . . . well, it holds something particular, doesn't it? To me, anyway. And I miss it. Something has been lost. And here I am, tapping out this endless email, perpetuating loss.

Anyway, to the evening. I had to deliver something to my neighbour, so went out into the wild wind and knocked.

We stood chatting. She's a great woman–a survivor with a sense of humour and true grit–the Duke again! She asked after my book, and suddenly began to describe the abuse her son had suffered at the hands of the priest around the corner. How he gave boys alcohol when they were not yet teens, and showed them inappropriate movies and . . .

Well. We know the story.

Again, as so often since the book came out–amazing how that one abuse story strikes at people–I am standing with someone who has been damaged, speaking in hushed (WHY hushed?) tones, about cruelty and abomination. I felt the wave of nausea it always brings.

Then there was a moment when we both felt the shift that had been created. I know this now. I can never unknow her sadness. But what to do with it?

I came home and opened up the computer. A habit. Writing is where I turn if I can't take a long walk. I found that email from my friend in the army, and wanted to weep. I won't send the full story. It is too sad. But the wages of war are even more than I'd imagined.

Then, instead of reading your stories of windswept brides and jazzy families, I made the mistake of opening

Dad's package. Photos, history and a letter. Such a letter. Delving into his own backstory for me. At one point, speaking of a moment of grief, the word 'We' was written, then crossed out.

That is what I mean about handwriting. He wanted to say more but restraint stepped in. No computer can do that. The moment of his loss, somehow suggested by a crossed-out pronoun.

Then I opened Brett's envelope.

In it was the book Mum made for us in her final months. I haven't read it since she died in 1994. We were a mess in so many ways–from the outside anyway–with divorces and step-siblings etc. But the love. And the loss of it. Of place and people. Ordinary loss. No holocausts or survivors or–thankfully–abuse. Just the loss of love.

And that, dear Antonio, was when I read your email. It made me try to rise out of my mire, and remember how I feel on the road when the world thrusts kindness after kindness at me. I loved picturing you all amid fields of green for a wedding, and then a party party party.

I shall think of you next Tuesday night as you and your parishioners attempt to make your way through to something like a glimmer of light in the morass that is 'the abuse disaster'. Practical love seems to me the thing to offer, though cool heads will be required more. You will combine both beautifully, I know. I have seen that.

I am intrigued by your 'pathological unease about religious language'. It makes me want to sneak in and listen to a sermon sometime. Your man–and now my man, I suspect–Richard Holloway talked of preachers as 'flowers that have the look of being looked at', and I know something of what he means from the theatre. I'd like to listen to your sermon when you didn't know I was there, because every person you know 'out front' must have some bearing on the words. How not?

I watched an echidna foraging in the bush for about ten minutes yesterday, and realised how blessed I was that he had no idea I was there. He almost walked across my boots. How rare and remarkable. I'd like to observe your sermon in just that way, so you felt no compunction to offer anything particular in service to a friend. Do you? Or is that an actor memory about having particular audience members in?

God language. A lifetime with it, and yet you try to hold yourself aside from it. I admire that. We so easily fall into the lingo of our world. We in showbiz do it all the time, daaahling!

Now I must quote you to yourself–'Excuse the length of this mail–you must be dropping off to sleep reading it.' I'm really sorry. This is turning from an essay into a thesis and I must let you off the hook. I am your drunk in the police station.

I'm going to sit with a cup of tea–yes, again!–and open the pages of Barry Oakley's book, for which so very many thanks. It just arrived.

No. First I'm going to look at the accompanying note, and print the shape of your handwriting into my memory. How could you have known when you penned it that you'd be satisfying a longing–to reclaim the shape of friends' hands. I will sit, sip tea, look at your spiky letters, and be thankful. The house is warm and quiet. I have solitude until my 2.30 pm meeting. Chuck this into the trash if you wish, but know, deep down, that you've given respite with your friendship. Here's to leaning towards each other over our broken gates.

A x

Never, ever, ever, apologise for your letters. What you sent me is a rare and beautiful gift. If I can find the way to reply with your language and insight I'll die a happy man.

Fuller response coming.

Tony

Tony,

Now that will be quite enough about you dying–happy or no. One of the things that occasionally sees me racing to my computer as the day begins is a little voice saying, 'Is he still breathing?' Sorry if that sounds like drama queen behaviour. But there it is. An irrational fear. So I'll thank you to keep the jokes about mortality for your swimming mates.

Here's something lovely to balance that nonsense . . .

I just now learned this.

Terimah kasih, which means 'thank you' in the language of Bali, translates as 'receive love.' Isn't that fascinating?

So, for being so generous about my interminable rave, here's a taste of my extraordinary poetic skill:

Terimah kasih, terimah kasih.
Terimah kasih, terimah kasih.
Terimah kasih, terimah kasih, terimah kasih,
Terimah kasih, terimah kasih.

OK. So I'm not giving up my day job.

Now I'm off to prep. Tonight is my last book gig for this year, and I'm going to say TERIMAH KASIH to some writers who changed my life.

Love,

Ailsa

PS For some time now, I have found myself wanting to sign off with the word 'love' at the end of these emails. But I hesitated. Why? I use the word with abandon with other chums, so why am I not using it with you? Is it, heaven forfend, a sin to express love to a Monsignor? Well, in my church the expression of love to a friend could never be a sin. And you, Antonio, are most definitely a friend, one who makes me expand. People speak of falling in love, but our friendship makes me rise, so I want to sign off as I feel, when I feel it. I hope that's not a problem for you. If it is, I suppose you will just have to squirm and bear it.

Ailsa,

Signing off with 'love' doesn't bring on the smallest of squirms. The word has been battered around in so many ways, but I really like your notion of 'rising in love'. Impressive new insight for me.

That response really is coming.

Thanks.

With the most sincere and respectful affection,

T

Tony–

So is Christmas!

Seriously, how can it be December?

No rush. Really. I'm such a gabbler.

Love,

A

Ailsa,

Let me go back and try to deal with things in chronological order.

I've been reflecting on that horrific story of your neighbour. The monster of sexual abuse seems to trail you like a bloodhound. I feel for you.

Nor is this monster very far from my own thoughts and feelings. When it's sheeted home to fellow priests, it tears me apart, and leaves a feeling of sickness in the pit of my stomach. It drains my confidence in the ideals of care and compassion which we are supposed to represent. It's an ugliness which is part of a mutilated world.

You know, I've no idea how many parishioners might come on Tuesday to express their confusion and raw emotions. There might be ten. There might be a hundred. There's no great complexity about such a meeting—just giving people with all of the hurt and distress they carry a safe place to express their real feelings.

Parishes are primarily about healing—first-aid stations for the spiritually wounded. Only hope that such a meeting, or continuing meetings for that matter, might provide a small step in that direction.

Wish me luck.

Now this is in no way a competition of who can write the longest email. You can reply to this in three short lines. When I start to write what's going on in my life—I must say there turns out to be a lot I want to tell you. I know it might be hard to convince you, but I am actually holding back.

Your letters, which you've dismissed as too hasty, too fast, skimming over the surface, are some of the most substantial letters I can recall ever receiving.

If that is surface stuff, my dear Ailsa, I'm not sure I could handle you at your most thoughtful philosophical best. The deep water.

There is a phrase that is bandied about called 'emotional intelligence' which I have never entirely understood. But if it means what I think it means—you are a person of exceptional emotional intelligence. Which I have to say I find intriguing and compelling.

I remember conversations I've had with another actor friend—actually, you met Paul when he came to dinner at your place—about the training regime that drama school graduates go through. The intensity of dealing with your own identity, the pursuit of self-awareness, trying to distinguish between what some scholars call the 'true self' and the 'false self' and all that stuff. And I came to realise what bloody hard work it can be.

The interesting crossover is with the training we went through in the seminary—for something they called 'the spiritual life'. Very similar dynamics. Not sure the methods and procedures we were introduced to worked too well. They had a hard edge to them. Was it the all-male environment we lived in? The celibacy? The isolated nature of our life tucked away in the seminary? Dunno. Perhaps I should have gone to acting school.

The idea of 'true self' and 'false self' I think is pretty central for anyone who seriously wants to develop a more spiritual life. Searching to be a more authentic person requires hard work. Talking simply, I guess it's our fears that create the masks we construct to hide our real self away from the gaze of others. Correct me if I'm wrong but I always think our most effective actors seem to be able to take on the role of another person if they are at home with themselves. The people who model a mature spiritual life for me seem to enjoy that same 'at homeness'.

Thanks for telling me about Louise and the delight you enjoy in one another. For the walking and talking and laughing and storytelling—I was hit with the conviction that women have more fun. Although on reflection I'm not sure that's entirely accurate. Perhaps a different shape to their fun. Whatever about these flights of fancy—I felt a tiny bit of jealousy, or perhaps envy is a better word (or even a mixture of both). I think you were talking about the same thing to me—sharing friends etc. Whatever about all of that—would love to meet her sometime.

Conversation—well, relationship, I guess—is a great mystery at times. I mean, who you feel comfortable opening up your life to, and who leaves you tongue-tied and guarded. The puzzle, for me at least, is that sometimes I feel more at ease with chance acquaintances or even total strangers than those I am closest to.

My brother Peter, the skinny kid in the rubber ring story I told you, is six years older than me and was always my hero and model in so many ways. But often, my adult conversations with him became jammed in some totally frustrating and strange way. Not unlike many Australian men, we would degenerate into stories of the most recent sporting news. I'm not suggesting the problem was simply on his side, though. Some deep sibling demon would frazzle my mind, leaving me with little to say. Strange stuff.

Recently, as he has been suffering from dementia, I've developed the habit of taking him for a Saturday drive, and to my utter delight something has loosened up in our conversation. It has became expansive, intimate and real. An absolute gift, given all that is being lost.

Last weekend, we drove down to Tambourine Bay. Aside from our swimming adventures, it was a favourite area of exploration for us as kids. Wading in mangrove mud up to our waists. Bird nesting. Catching locusts. Navigating an old and leaky tin canoe.

As we sat looking across to where the baths used to be,

we were kids again. The years fell away like leaves in a gentle breeze. Each fought to get into the conversation. We reminisced about past sporting glories, told the inevitable lies, and boasted outrageously without fear of offence—or of anyone contradicting us. It was like a dam bursting its walls. We laughed until our eyes were wet.

I will hold onto that memory, because we've been having very disturbing days with him lately. He's in hospital after a fall. Tough time for us all. He is such a rock for me—my hero brother. Strange how you never throw off the roles of childhood, no matter how ancient you become. With Christmas looming I suppose the family will be celebrating with the 'hats and the pudding' in the aged care place Pete's in. That'll be a first. Not quite sure how I'll handle it. I feel a strong responsibility to make it right.

How do you pronounce TERIMAH KASIH? Are there Indonesian phrases in your box of tricks? Spanish, Italian, French, Balinese—what is this uncommonly gifted woman yet capable of? I'm trying like crazy to keep up with the 'new steps', as Baz Luhrmann would say. Did I ever tell you I was on the radio once with Tara Morice? Couldn't help myself asking her for a dance as I whistled 'Time After Time'.

No more nonsense. Love showing off. Don't think any less of me. I simply should have been a really bad actor—but somehow stumbled into another profession.

Hope 'your' Peter is travelling well.

Happy days, and buckets of Bali love.

Tony

PS Keep thinking of other topics—such as the loss of actual letters and handwriting. Another time.

DEAR READER,

When we looked back on our letters, Ailsa was shocked at how often we had returned to the issue of death and dying. For me, I suppose, there was less surprise, because death is a professional constant of my working week. Nonetheless when I read that account of taking Peter to Tambourine Bay, I was thrown back to the days around his death. Peter let go of his life four months after that email.

He died in hospital after weeks of a difficult and crucial struggle, early one soft April morning. He was alone.

Late the night before, his wife Margaret and I had broken our long bedside vigil and returned home to snatch some sleep. Called back to the hospital near dawn, the family sat around his bed in loving silence, remembering stories of his life in floods of tears mixed with nose-running laughter, and praying familiar words from our childhood. Finally I anointed his dead body, the man with whom I had been bonded at the hip for eight decades.

Brothers have many languages, some of which are physical like bruises and broken fingers, and punching each other when you want to say I love you but don't know how to say it right; some of them are the gentle and not-so-gentle put-downs the Irish call 'slagging'; some of them involve competing in sporting contests—for us it was golf—as though lives depended upon the outcome. Many languages—even at times, those that employ words.

On that morning, as his younger brother, I anointed him with the ancient sacrament of farewell and with my tears. As I've already mentioned in an email, the Catholic ritual directs the celebrant to trace a small cross in oil on the head, the heart, the ears, the eyes, each hand and foot—reverencing the dead body. This ancient language of human touch becomes a dramatic acknowledgement of the sacred and heroic journey of each person. Words of farewell are to be spoken gently.

Peter died of dementia. Such patients die slowly, life leaking away like water from a cracked kettle. His last weeks were spent in hospital. His language was confused and his thoughts rambled along ever-wilder paths. Any attempt at even the simplest conversation was too hard. We smiled a lot. Sometimes he smiled back. Toughest of all was when his frustration and anger became so intense that the medical staff had to attach restraints to hold him in bed for his own safety. We were left emotionally shredded.

To deal with my grief, I developed the habit of massaging his feet and his restless legs with soothing oil. For me, and I confidently believe for Peter himself, it was a moment of intense connection and love. Funny thing—I suppose like many men of our age, we rarely expressed our affection for one another in any physical manner. None of this hugging business. Wrestling perhaps, in the backyard; being 'doubled' on the back of our ancient bicycle; or packing down in a rugby scrum, were all acceptable behaviours, even the stuff of heroes. Hugging, no way! And yet here we were experiencing the deep, primitive magic of touch. 'Touch comes before sight, before speech,' observes Canadian writer Margaret Atwood. 'It is the first language and the last, and it always tells the truth.' I didn't fully realise at the time that I was rehearsing what was to become a deeper reality in the sacrament of his last anointing.

Grief is the price we pay for love. If you don't want to grieve, don't love. My parents' deaths were separated by 25 years. To have been with each of them at the moment they died I regard as a special grace. It is scarcely necessary to spell out, but there is something heartrending about anointing your parents and then praying for them over their graves.

Dealing with ongoing grief is another thing—at least that has been my experience. For my mother I keep telling stories about her colourful life—to anyone or any group who will listen. Twenty years on I tell and retell them, again and again. Her wonderfully acerbic sense of humour, her love of horse racing and politics, her unfashionable yet strong paintings (a skill she only discovered in her old age), her Irish love of whisky and milk.

'What whisky and milk can't cure,' she would say, 'can't be cured.'

For my father, when I recovered from the first wound of letting him go, I went off on a determined search to find the story of his father and his father's father. Finally I uncovered a fabulous tale of love and survival.

To lose a brother, however, is quite different. It is to have a limb amputated. The sweet memories of our childhood adventures choked me. Four years on, I still miss him keenly. There may come a future time, perhaps, when telling his stories will help to lubricate my grief. Not yet.

In the Catholic funeral service—the Requiem Mass— there is a phrase that never fails to have me catch my breath, that sits in the midst of prayers which are sometimes more florid yet contain less impact:

'Life is changed, not ended.'

A phrase stark in its simplicity; words which capture generations of Christian belief, quite devoid of the sometimes frantic claims of believers about the mystery of death.

On this day I was celebrating my own brother's farewell. Questions were never far below the surface of my mind, as this moment of letting go gripped me in a vice. Are we no more than accidental creatures in an accidental universe? Are our prayers simply a childish search for security or are they a genuine search for truth? In the face of death, are our prayers merely the noise of deluded and frightened people? Is the sacred story of my brother's life simply a journey 'full of sound and fury, signifying nothing'?

Sometimes Christian believers appear to be free of confusion about death. That is not my personal experience. Faith should never be confused with certainty. Belief and knowledge are two quite different ways of seeing. I do not *know* what happens when a human being dies. I do not *know* where this gift of human consciousness in a newborn baby comes from. In short, I don't know where we came from, nor do I know where we go when we die.

But amidst the sound and the fury of our life, all the tragedy and at times senselessness of it, for some of us there exists a gentle whisper of belief, a rumour of angels, a treasured story passed down by those who love us.

We *believe* that we come from the hands of a gentle and loving mystery we call our God. We *believe* that finally we return to those tender hands, which gave us the gift of life in the first place, into the most merciful of all embraces.

Life is changed, not ended.

One of the tragic but inevitable facts of life, is that we die with more beauty in us than we have ever been able to express; with more imagination than people have ever been able to see; with more dreams than our family and friends have ever heard; with a more beautiful song in us than we have ever been able to sing. We are all unfinished symphonies.

Peter is one of those unfinished symphonies.

His music, my faith assures me, will, in some entirely mysterious manner, continue to enrich my life and all those who love him.

Tony

Tony!

Big news!

As of the 13th of December, Peter and I will be in Ubud, where we plan to spend Christmas. I will have WiFi, but am NOT taking my computer. So my request to you, oh best of pen-pals, is that you might continue to jot me some lines, despite the fact that I may not be able to answer as fully as usual. Call me pushy, but please say yes.

Now. Back to your missive from over a broken gate . . .

Thanks for your generosity about what I wrote. 'Emotional intelligence' is an oft-used term in the theatre, too. Like you I'm never sure what it is or who has it, but I think that if I'm going to claim any kind of intelligence, that might be the one I'd want. It's more practical than any other, I'll wager. And practical—useful—is the thing I'd most like to be.

The seminary training . . .

All the things you mention—celibacy, isolation, separation from the opposite sex—seem to me to be recipes for hard outcomes, to be honest. Interestingly, though, there are similarities between life in the theatre and religious life, despite the fact that those edges don't exist in showbiz.

I think the strongest in both worlds respond to some kind of calling, even if they resist it being categorised that way, but I'm sure that fragile people can be damaged by entering theatre or seminary. Much of it has to do with the way in which creativity calls to be expressed in all of us. When that is stopped up or denied, it's no surprise to me that despair or depression follow. We see those, along with alcoholism and substance abuse, among the clergy, but they also occur in the theatre, in no small part because of the long periods of enforced unemployment. Being unable to express creatively can be a kind of death.

I realise that some traditions hold that creativity and celibacy are linked, but I'm of the mind that creativity and sexual expression rise from the same centre in the body—and from what I've observed, if the possibility for creation is denied, that will lead to hard outcomes.

You write of true and false selves, and I take your point, though having investigated all manner of characters in my work, I'm not so sure that such things exist.

Actors work to inhabit other selves, many of them seemingly a world away. In the process, what most good actors do is uncover aspects of themselves that might help to reveal the puzzle of the character's journey. Inevitably, actors come to empathise with the person they're playing. They don't become them, but they do get to see the world through other eyes.

This strikes me as an important lesson for life. We are all capable of having a sociopath self or a saintly self, depending on the way 'given circumstances' hit us. Personally, I don't think that 'the self' is static—that there can be a true and false version of it. Rather, I think the self is constantly evolving, and I'm not sure how much we can ever know it—know our self. But the search for self—the examination and consideration and discovery of our whys and wherefores—is the only way through this turbulent life on our messy planet. Ha! We're back to Holloway and his monster and saint in a mutilated world! Or perhaps to the old gem about the unexamined life being not worth living.

The aside to all that is—no, I don't think people have to be self-realised in order to be great actors. Rather, they have to be permeable. Thin-skinned. Open. Wide open. They have to be prepared to let the 'stuff' of life in and out without much protection. Consider many of the greatest actors—people I would almost call shamans in that their gifts were so luminous. Some were alcoholics and depressives, violent at times, or mean. No naming names, but you don't have to look far to find them. Genius—or the great actor's gift of revelation—has a cost. Interestingly, though, many of my favourites are, anecdotally at least, sane and balanced in their personal lives, able to manage fame, and the need to morph, with grace and sanity.

As to women having more fun in life, Antonio—well believe it or not, I don't have an opinion on that, but I know I have more than my allotted share!

I'm so very sorry to hear about your brother. Dementia is vicious, and it trades on fear and guilt. We went through it a little with Peter's mum, and so I know something of the journey. I can well imagine it will create pain for your family, and I have nothing useful to offer you save for my sympathy. Are you trying to fix, Tony? Is it fixable? Or is it just that you want to love as much as possible for as long as possible? They may be different impulses. Not preaching to the preacher–that would be impudent and too silly. Just asking. Wondering. Hoping you are not setting yourself up for heartbreak. Families are the ultimate teachers, are they not? That fierce, uncontestable love that proclaims itself– first, last, blood, history . . . swimming rings . . .

'Christmas looming.'

I'm glad I will be in a place where offerings are made daily at doorways and by riverbanks and on hillsides. Where the idea of divine is built with flowers and little biscuits and palm fronds and incense. Where *terimah kasih*–receive love–is on every set of lips, and the smiles never stop.

I don't speak Bahasa, sadly. How I wish. But I'd wager there is nowhere on earth where the smile is spoken so clearly, and the language of the heart so readily adopted. And there are few places I've been where 'God language' is as unnecessary, because God is lived in the daily activities with such effort-less grace. It's a place where I can truly give thanks.

I wish you were here to come for a walk with me. The thing about walking in company is that it teaches compromise. To find the rhythm of another. To adjust. To share silence and talk. To listen. And I slow down then. I can do slow, you know. Maybe it's not as much fun as whistling for Tara Morice, but more fun than whistling Dixie!

Tomorrow I will do a food shop at my favourite Italian supermarket, because I'm cooking for ten on Saturday night. They are predicting THIRTY-SEVEN degrees on Saturday and so I must prep as much as I can.

I think it a very good thing you didn't become an actor. Show-offs are not what we need in our biz.

Much, much, so much to discuss. And I must stop.

Gracias, Tony. I will carry you as I walk. Your brother's illness, along with all else for which you feel 'responsible', must make the days heavy sometimes.

Swim strong, *compañero*.

A x

Ailsa,

Just back from a funeral, and lacking energy to respond as I'd wish. But a story rose to the surface, when you admitted—to my relief—that you didn't speak Bahasa as well as those other lingos. Always thought it a chancy business trying to remember bits and pieces of a language not our own. I heard of a man once who claimed he could say in Swahili, 'I have two oranges.' Always seemed a slender base for further conversation.

I buried a friend a few months ago, an inveterate traveller who maintained it was vital to know one phrase in as many languages as possible, especially for use in high-priced restaurants. The phrase?

'My friend will pay.'

I pass it on to you. The only wisdom I can summon just now.

Must put my head down. Will write when I can do justice to your thoughts.

T

Antonio.

I'm wasted—but not in the way that you are. I don't know how you manage all those funerals. To call it 'part of the job' as you do is deliberately underplaying it, I know. It must cost.

Anyway, my exhaustion rises from a conversation that left me raging. This time with a Professional Devout Catholic. She claims the abuse stories are over-dramatised. I can't cop that party line. Too defensive by half. I won't go any further, save to say that I feel I want to curl in a ball like a wounded dog and lick wounds. How do you do it, friend?

Hope I didn't offend or give hurt by questioning you about your brother. Been thinking about it on and off all night. What would I know? Would I have included those questions if I had written by hand? Not sure.

My brothers, Brett and Justin, are touchstones for me in very different ways, and to entertain the thought of losing them, even for a moment, is to cause instant pain. I'm so sorry for any stress caused by impudence or thoughtlessness. Hope the water was soothing this morn. Please tell me if I gave hurt. I mean it.

Oh dear. Neurotic blonde.

Write blog. Prune roses. Clean bathroom. Chop wood. Carry water.

Send love.

Sign off.

A x

PS I love your friend's advice about learning 'My friend will pay'. What a guy. Brilliant. I have consulted Google Translate, and they have given me the Indonesian version. Hopefully it will get me across the line–*Teman saya akan membayar*. Thanks!

Hope you are resting well.

Good God woman. Hurt me?!!

You mean about giving me your loving sage advice about Peter?

You can't be serious.

It was received as you sent it—with affection, good sense and all the marks of a genuine intriguing *compañera*. I'm left with a deep sense that our friendship grows and matures with every conversation. One of these days I'll give you cause to really beat me up (I'd better put some sort of smiley badge on that statement, like they do—but can't find one). And I trust that such an event will only help us break through to yet another level of this pilgrimage.

Professional Devout Catholic.

Yes, of course they exist, but I'm put in mind of the words of Dan Berrigan, the fabled Jesuit activist. He used to say to those who enquired why he remained a priest when everyone else had left, that 'many of the worst people on planet earth that I know are Catholic. But it just happens that some of the best people I know, share this same tradition. They give me strength.' (Rough translation by me)

That insight gives me strength.

The gospel story of the wheat and the weeds comes to mind.

This, of course, is not an answer to the many issues you raised in your last mail. I have to find some more creative space to do it justice. Just had a long meeting with the parish finance committee and my brain is fried. Also, as the old bumper sticker says—Procrastinate NOW!

Night night.

Tony

PS Thanks for your sensitivity to this spiky echidna. I like to think of myself as pretty rugged and invulnerable actually. However, today I spent a couple of hours with Peter. He's not travelling too well, and your words make great sense.

Good morning, rugged invulnerable one. I'm so sorry to hear about Peter. It's very tough when we can't make things better.

Selfishly, relief flooded in and a little something lifted. I had not wanted to be impertinent. Thank you. Really. Phew.

But don't kid yourself. The echidna's only defence is to tuck its head under, roll into a ball, and hope the predator can't be bothered. Rugged? Not!

You know, it's a toss-up as to whether I love them or the snail more. I think the echidna's gait is entirely captivating–that rolling, comic walk, snuffling along. And the self-absorption. And the lack of awareness of anything but the thing they must do and be.

The snail, of course, is my favourite, and probably my necessary totem.

Silly talk.

I was thinking about what gift to make to the multitude tonight when we break bread. The others at table will be two women writers, two actors (one of them Pete, of course), a theatre designer, an art historian, and three folk with connections into the visual art world. I'm in awe of all of them. Perhaps a poem at each place would be good.

I'm readying to go and walk with Louise (the other actor who will be at table!) before breakfast. The north wind is already fierce. Swim like an echidna–but remember, they have no resistance to anything.

A x

Didn't think those bloody spikes were working.

Eddie the Echidna

PS Did you have any notion that on the Saturday morning you visited my home, on the table (carefully positioned between us) was a small plastic fridge magnet echidna. Been there for weeks—without me paying any attention. Whence it came—only the Phantom do know!

Pilgrim,

Your instructions, should you choose this assignment, are to matter-transport yourself to Hamilton St so you can be at this table I am preparing. You would love it. I'm copying off poems and scattering flowers and feeding a fatted calf. I will put a poem out for you.

By the way, your thoughts on the word PIOUS?

I was driving home and decided that 'pious' was the opposite of Louise and something I never want to be.

Am I showing ignorance of something wonderful that has been lost?

A x

Ailsa,

As usual our emails crossed the Murray about the same time. I wonder if they wave to one another.

Let me tell you a closely guarded secret—I stand in awe of intelligent female writers and would be reduced to an incoherent mumble in such a group. My entire resources are focused on keeping my secret safe from one highly intelligent author.

HowamIdoin?

I'm off to a wedding—the bride can't be kept waiting.

Ant

Hope that bride wasn't tapping her feet. Mary Oliver wrote a bride poem which is my mantra. Words to live by. Google it and see why. It's called 'When Death Comes'.

I am bursting-at-the-seams happy. I've had a whole day playing with flowers, fruit, vegetables, poems and places at table, and dreaming up ways to fete my friends. I'm a feeder. I love to sit in candlelight and hear arguments and laughter and watch those I love become full. And I've adored the prep, in spite of the fact that it's thirty-seven degrees. I'm singing to Paul Simon and dancing from task to task in the ugliest outfit I own—and that's saying something! My falling-apart T-shirt and shorts are old friends with many memories in their fibres, and I won't abandon them. And now I'm trusting the clouds that are building to the west—let them bring me a cool change from my birthplace. I will think of it as a Fremantle doctor.

This is a postcard that reads 'Wish You Were Here.'

A x

Good morning.

Hungover?? Repairing a shattered house? Out walking, tasting again the memories of rich friendships and shimmering minds? Or still asleep?

Thought of you this morning while talking to my fellow travellers at Mass. I was quoting Thomas Merton: 'The biggest human temptation … is to settle for too little.' Let me assure you that this is one temptation you have beaten to a frazzle. Never could it be said of this explorer of the human condition and explorer of the road. Hope last night was as wonderful as you imagined.

Tony

And good morning to you, Eddie!

How are the spikes? Are you bristling? Or are you happily occupied, digging ever-deeper into the earth? Did you swim the swim of the happy echidna?

No, no, not hungover, unless you count an adrenaline detox.

Peter is doing the last round of dishes, and I've been reading two books in between doing some work. Rather wish I was still asleep, but lying in is something my constitution doesn't enjoy. Five hours is what my body allows before it starts agitating–much to Pete's dismay, at times. And so, in spite of rising yesterday at 5.30 and not turning in until 3, I rose at 7 and have been padding about the house, inhaling flowers grown by friends, responding to emails and texts as the others surfaced, and trying to decide what to do with today and tomorrow.

Anyway, it's blissfully cool, so I can choose and know that whatever I do, it will be easy. But to last night . . .

I was so moved by my friends, old and new. This year has been a battle between my extrovert and introvert selves. I've been away so much, feeling an overwhelming desire to meet and thank readers of my book, and to bring my best to them, wherever I meet them. But that has often left me without time or energy for my nearest and dearest, those who made it possible for me to go questing, secure in the knowledge that my home village was underneath me, buoying me. I've felt guilty about them, hungry for them, angry at myself for not being able to manage more people, but desperate too for the silence that is vital.

So yesterday was a distillation of all I had missed.

The day began with rhubarb, which set me up for my walk with Louise. Fast, ripping into the hot wind as we bowled around Albert Park Lake, talking a thousand to the dozen and rebuffing the northerlies. God, I love walking with her. We go at the world as we go at life.

Home and into the prep! Bare feet on floorboards, chopping, dicing, planning, prepping, singing, dancing. Up to my study to forage in my postcard collection for images for the table, which Peter hired from a party shop because ours would never have stretched to ten people. Gardenias and tea-lights in glass holders. Poems at each place. It looked so pretty.

In the kitchen . . .

I decided on a loosely Italian theme, because it's the cooking I know best. I learned it when I went there at twenty–a Perth kid, amazed by what they did with flowers and veges. With everything. Here is what was plated in six heavenly hours of kitchen play . . .

Antipasto . . .

Grilled eggplant and radicchio. Asparagus with buffalo mozzarella. Broad beans with mint and saltbush leaves. Marinated anchovies and Sicilian sardines. Button mushrooms and multicoloured radishes. Zucchini cream—a bit spicy so beware. Salami with fennel and chilli bought at a local farmers' market. How lucky are we?

Served with laughter and prosecco.

Within fifteen minutes of folk arriving, I was in the kitchen chopping mint when I looked up and thought I would burst—laughter, stories, hilarity, and most of the guests had only just met! So by the time we got to the table, you can imagine how things were flowing. All those amazing people, tumbling about each other, picking up the odd postcard and sharing stories about it and themselves, nibbling at my handiwork. Fellowship in motion.

Mains . . .

Fennel and pork sausages roasted in the oven with apple, red onion, beetroot and rosemary. Beyond description.

Cous-cous with orange rind, currants, Ras el Hanout spice mix (diverting from Italy), pine nuts and almonds. Oh, parsley thrown through, too!

Green beans and greener broccolini, separated by deep purple carrots. Pretty and pretty darned good.

We talked. We talked. We talked.

Dessert . . .

Meringues folded through cream whipped with vanilla (Pete may have a severe case of RSI from this task), then served with diced strawberries and a dollop of ginger rhubarb.

Cheese. Dried figs. Grapes. Quince jelly. Breads.

GRATITUDE.

More talk.

Laughter. Mime. History. Tall tales. Affection.

Friendship cannot be taken for granted—it requires nurturing. And that takes time. Well, yesterday I gave it time, with so much happiness and pleasure, and how it rewarded me. When finally we called it a night at 2 am, and Peter and I replayed the evening as we did a few dishes and packed away food, I realised that an entire day devoted to feeding and delighting the people I love may well have been the most creative thing I've done in weeks. Every bit of me felt full. Not with food, I don't mean that. For all that outrageous list of edibles, it wasn't a heavy or bloated night. We filled each other, and I felt blessed to have broken such bread.

I must go and decide about my day. I have a feeling this chair, this desk, this screen, will claim me. Even if I don't write much, I just love the idea of being in the house post-dinner, and soaking up some of the energies that are still floating about. Not to mention staring at the vases of flowers that fill the place. Hydrangeas are such decadent blooms. I want to look at them and feel rich.

Thank you for thinking of me in relation to the Merton. Sometimes in the little there is majesty, but 'to settle for'–that is the toxic phrase, isn't it? I also like whoever it was who said we never regret what we do, only the things we don't do.

I run on too long. I go, I go–see how I go.

Love,

Ailsa x

Good morning Ailsa,

Well you said you were an early morning person. So am I.

Just heading for the healing waters of the harbour before a proper reply to the pageantry and passion of your party.

It's raining here. Swimming in the rain is a special treat.
Happy days.
Tony

A

Now I'm flying out the door. The first tee calls.
T

T!

The first tee, indeed. What a frivolous sort of creature you are, splashing then chipping. And don't give me the philosopher-golfer stance. I don't buy it. It's all greens and crashing waves and frolic with you.

Hit well–or whatever one says to you addicts of the putt.

I'm staying at the desk. Will keep an eye for the early bird's missives.

Love from the snail on her trail . . .

Ailsa

Dear Ailsa,

Have I ever told you adequately what joy I get from your mail?

I go around here smiling my head off and when asked what this is all about—I haven't been able to find a way of telling them it is this blithe spirit in Victoria who brings poetry and light into my otherwise dull existence.

I end up mumbling something about indigestion.

They remain unconvinced.

No—haven't been drinking. Well perhaps one or two.

Where to start a proper reply?

First your description of *Babette's Feast* has me copying down the recipes.

But how could I serve it with the zest and playfulness of such a host? And besides I can't dance and cook at the same time. For me a far more serious endeavour.

In one sense you didn't have to describe in words the utter joy you felt at having such friends around you and dazzling them with your vivacious hospitality. I sensed it in the language. Can't remember reading such undiluted happiness.

Must go to bed.

Eddie

Hello Tony,

It's 5.43 am, and I'm beginning to fear long draughts of sleep will never again be mine. I didn't go to bed until about 12.30 am.

Thank you for saying my mails make you smile. I worry that this avalanche of correspondence is 'too much'. All my life, 'too much' has been the fear, and sometimes the catch-cry. I'm grateful you're not folding under the load.

You know, I'm not a 'true believer' in much. I loved that newly learned phrase you gave me by virtue of Bishop Holloway's book–'agnostic Christian'. As you know from my book, I've always longed to believe, to claim faith in the way of those old ladies in the Spanish churches, but the only faith I can claim is in working and walking and the wonder of here and now. And I was so relieved to hear him speak, your Richard Holloway, about the Jesus with whom he can sit comfortably, and the other, who is owned by the Church. Much of what he said was like a balm.

Sorry.

Back on the road, not the side tracks.

Dawn has come and gone while I've been writing. I have a 9.30 voiceover, which will bring me some actual lucre. Hooray! I don't think about it much, because there is no point in walking down a road that makes me frightened or miserable or envious–I don't enjoy being that person who feels those things–but I am so grateful when income finds me.

OK, Eddie. Prickle up, shuffle off and get to work.

Terimah kasih from the deep south.

A x

Ailsa,

I often wonder about how you manage to balance finances and work and life. How you deal with rejection and the constant pressure to produce—whether that pressure is external or internal. The artist's life seems to me to be one of constantly exercising a kind of faith—as you say, 'faith in work'. But there must be days when it falters. You speak of them rarely, but I am sure they are painful, so I thought you might be glad of this ...

My morning prayer for Ailsa.
May those who love us, love us.
And those who don't
May God turn their hearts.

And if God doesn't turn their hearts

May he turn their ankles.

So that we recognise them

In their limping.

Amen to that.

Ant

Antonio!

What a prayer! Thank you. I love it. And in return, here
is one for you . . .

My morning prayer for Tony.

For days that begin with crossing wires

For mornings that ring with the laughter of recognition

For a friend who turns up and puts in, every day

I give thanks.

I lift my croaky voice and join the cockatoos,

squarking my good fortune to the tumbling sky.

May blessings rain on you, spiky swimmer.

A x

Ailsa

Your letter arrived in today's mail. You're right. A hand-written letter is entirely different. Must say I thought you a tiny bit romantic talking about the distinction between a handwritten letter and email. Let me withdraw my scepti-cism with some embarrassment.

So. How is your handwritten letter different to your email?

More vulnerable, stronger feelings, and even a touch more human.

Thanks for the stories about your dad. Loved what you wrote—'a gentle man and a gentleman.' I realised that I had never asked you about him. Good to get a bit more Piper backstory.

So much to say in response to your questions about my

father. To commence—with apologies for not writing by hand!

Dad was 39 when I was born. A little older than some dads when I was growing up. As I write this, I realise that, when he died, he was six years younger than I am now.

Like yourself, he held few values higher than friendship. His family and his friends were what mattered. Unlike his more enterprising wife, the loftier ambitions like income or owning your own home were unimportant. They were both ardent party givers. To us kids there seemed to be a shindig most Saturday nights. Either home or away. He expressed his affection easily. A little sentimental at times, I guess. Had no hesitation at greeting women with an enthusiastic hug. Thank God the habit was not hereditary.

As I've mentioned before, as a nineteen-year-old, Dad enlisted for the Great War. After experiencing the horror of France, Dad was invalided from the front.

When he died in 1972 I went before an ex-servicemen's tribunal in an attempt to win a war widow's pension for Mum. The challenging task was to prove Dad died of war injuries 54 years after they were first inflicted. It took some careful argument. To make the case, it fell on me to research a period of his life, before I was born, of which I knew precious little. I had to stretch my imagination to collect the story: my parents never owned their own home; never owned a car; never had more than a few bob to bless themselves with. What their Saturday night parties lacked in lavish catering was made up for with loud music, and enthusiastic singing. They were never dull.

Despite all that lack, they conjured up bursaries for Peter and me at Riverview.

Caught up by the private school culture of entitlement, I developed a horrible case of being disappointed by my NSW Railway draughtsman father. My future was going to be the stock market and Pitt St—striped ties and double breasted suits. In a word, I was simply a prick of a son.

My research developed, with me feeling increasingly ashamed, as the picture of their life continued to emerge ...

A young man shipped off to the war to end all wars. Coming home quite shattered, getting married, not having enough money to have a decent honeymoon, caught up in the Depression of 1929. And then another war. I have strong memories of his coming home during WWII after working three jobs, now a civilian, grey-faced with fatigue, touching on exhaustion. Experienced manpower was at a premium.

The tribunal allowed me to argue the case for a full hour— the best hour I have ever spent. I had realised the dimension of my father's real story for the first time. It was heroic. It filled me with a deep shame at how frequently I had underestimated what I owed him. What we all owed him.

This led me on to a determined search for my Irish roots. To discover my father's father. Too long to tell you tonight but (for me) equally fascinating.

What the hell. Here's a taste of it.

Can't help myself.

Have I ever told you that Dad had the most elegant handwriting? You'd have loved it. He was a professional draughtsman. Not only that, he had a hobby creating what the Irish would call illuminated text—think the Book of Kells. For him, designing the most elaborate letters in the tradition of the Celtic monks in their 'beehive' cells was a passion. One eerie coincidence arising from our family history is that St Columcille, the giant figure in Irish tradition and the person responsible for the Book of Kells, was born in the same tiny Donegal village where Dad's grandparents lived.

How's that for genetic inheritance?

To get back to your handwritten letter, though.

Can I tell your future from your handwriting? No! But from everything else that is happening to you I believe you are powering along. It's an exciting ride simply being caught in the wash.

Had our parish meeting tonight about the sexual abuse issue. It provided a safe space for all of us to express our dismay, emotional turmoil and confusion. Everyone was generous and honest in their responses. It went well. The people who came showed such openness and adulthood. I felt very lucky to be part of this community.

I really experienced your love and support. It was strangely tangible. Thanks.

What time do you leave for Bali?

Much love,

Tony

Dear Tony,

Thank you. I needed those stories.

No reason in particular. Just a long day. I think, too, I was holding some weird tension about your meeting. 'Carrying' for you, though you had not asked it, and I had no right.

I am bone weary so this will be short.

I'm glad the letter arrived. Of course I forgot that the thing I rue about snail mail is that I can't look back and see what I wrote. Letters are in and of their moment—unless you are a person who thinks to keep copies. That isn't me. So you now have a piece of me that I will never get back.

A couple of years ago I bundled up swags of letters and returned them as gifts. Friends were overwhelmed. They got back many moments of their lives that had been forgotten. So keep that little piece of me safe, please.

Thank you for the story of your dad. Such hopes. All that wishing for you and your brother. All that work. You are the living legacy, and he would be proud, I'm sure. Also good to know there was happiness and friendship. Important to know it was not all loss or sadness.

What was his name, your Da?

And the meeting . . .

I'm relieved for you. I hope all were able to go into the night feeling something like peace. You're admirable for giving people the opportunity and for creating a safe space.

We leave for Bali on Thursday morning at 9.30 am. At the airport by about 7. Leave home by 6.15 or so. Note to self. Book a cab!

I have one more day in which to organise my life. I'm in need of the break, and looking forward, but I'm having pre-partum anxiety, I think.

Compañero. How many words are there for gratitude? I send thanks and love. Also to your father's memory, and to your brother and sister. Which is to say—to you. I hope you three living legacies hold each other tight in the coming days and weeks.

A x

Dear Ailsa,

What did you mean when you said you 'had no right' to feel for me and the parishioners in the abuse meeting? Surely friendship gives you sufficient right to 'carry' for me. Your stated credo (in your book) speaks of the importance of taking responsibility for one another. That's what you were doing, wasn't it?

And I'm grateful.

You know, it's not easy to cherry-pick the most important moments out of eight packed decades. But I realise that I have never told you this story, and it is one of the most important of my life.

Settle back with your slippers, please ...

I was quite a latecomer to the passionate—and fashionable!—search for family roots. It had sort of passed me by. I never fantasised about being related to Hannibal or any of his elephants, nor had I grown up with any sense of Irishness. But once I joined the club there was no stopping me.

First went to Ireland from the US in the summer of 1976. After exploring both the South and the North, and being totally seduced by a culture familiar beyond words, I came away with a deeper understanding of myself than I had ever before fathomed. But try as I may I couldn't discover anything about my original family in Donegal.

Eight years later, back home, a historian in Melbourne unveiled the saga you already know that brought my great-grandparents to Australia. He insisted that I return to Donegal, organise a service in memory of those evicted with my family, contact the press and the local universities, and make sure there was a Protestant minister with me to share the service. And as an afterthought to raise the money to fund the whole project! All this happened in the brevity of a telephone conversation. I was left stunned looking at the phone, wondering about the dimension of what I had said yes to.

Unbelievably, it all came to pass.

The memorial service for the Derryveagh refugees took place in a soft late summer twilight on the banks of a beautiful Donegal lough, 118 years after the scandalous eviction. We sang songs, told stories, listened to the music of the fiddle and piano accordian, recited the names of the 112 families made homeless, read poetry and prayed—and then retreated to McClafferty's pub.

A historian once said to me—'Ireland is the land of your imagination.'

I understood his words for the first time on the banks of that lough. The experience gave me a new sense of who I was.

Tony

My dear Tony,

The fan blades are tick tick ticking over my head, but the air they are pushing down is hot. I'm in training for Bali. The gods are assisting me with my transition. This time tomorrow I'll be under another fan, under another roof, under another sky. Or maybe I'll be under the water of a pool, listening to *gamalan* and prayers drifting over the wall from the temple. There'll be incense rising somewhere from a freshly placed offering–by a door, on a path, at an intersection. Intersections are important. The smells will be intense–that curious mixture of frangipani, smoke and sewage that is the tropics. Life and death. Ripening and rotting.

I've done all my work, save for our annual Christmas card photo. I have not much heart for it, this year, but I will do it out of ritual, and because it's a kept promise. So expect at least one more missive this evening. Other than that, my final blog post is written. I have prepped and photo-copied my readings for the in-conversation I'm doing in Ubud—Books That Changed My Life. No surprises. Garner and Oliver. And Mary Grant Bruce's Billabong books. It was hard to pass up Kipling's *Just So Stories*. His 'best beloved' with the 'satiable curiosity' was a passion. I thought he was writing all those yarns for me.

For reading, I will raid our friends' library and let myself go wherever their shelves lead. For writing I will buy exercise books at the supermarket.

Oh, Tony. I'm so sorry.

I just realised I should have responded to your Irish story at the beginning of this letter. You must be wondering if I read a word you said. Good grief, talk about self-obsessed. Really. Not good enough. So sorry.

It is a very moving reflection, and I can almost smell the thick grass and hear the fiddle. Isn't it intriguing that both of us have these profound experiences of 'going back' to a kind of mythic heartland of the ancestors? Yours, of course, had ritual around it and gave you re-connection to the community of your forebears. I can see how that might have remade you, or at least, shown you aspects of yourself that you had not examined previously. My recent return to the Gascoyne was rather more haphazard, and it is still too fresh to make a lot of sense, but there is something that resonates when I wonder what it might have been that drove my forebears to want to walk hundreds of miles to claim stretches of that desert. I guess maybe it was the thrill of having land. The possibilities must have seemed endless.

But it's more than that. I read a kind of restlessness from them into myself. That yearning to walk further, seek another view. I recognise that. Just as I recognise the fervour of that Piper ancestor of mine, the Bible Christian Pastor. Perhaps I'm a mix of evangelist and wanderer! Bit dangerous!

Of course it's way too soon to draw any conclusions or even understanding from my recent voyage and discoveries, but your story makes me see how such learnings, particularly when they involve seeing actual sites of family story, can re-form us.

Anyway, a huge apology for prattling on about myself before mentioning your offering. My only excuse–a flabby one, as you would say–is that it has been quite a day. Not sure I can articulate it really. There is something strange going on inside me. Like a kind of apprehension about leaving my work at such an early stage. An odd sadness often comes upon me as Christmas looms–I use that word advisedly. It is such a swirl of commercial jingoism, and it makes me feel very much an outsider because I don't want *stuff* in vast quantities, or piles of food, or to go to endless parties with people I barely know.

Sorry. Such a curmudgeon. I will try to keep my grump-iness to myself, this being a time of year when you must be feeling joyous. I do recognise that the story that gives us all this season is a lovely one–that baby surrounded by silence and awe and soft-faced sheep. But I am rarely able to get to anything like that amid the lunacy of presents.

I want presence.

And time.

Oh for heaven's sake! I am going to bed. Should delete this message but am about to hit send, because the apology is necessary. I will never treat one of your

314

stories that way again–certainly not a story about your father.

Lo siento.

The Spanish for 'sorry' translates to 'I feel it'. And I do.

Hope your head is on a pillow, and your eyes are closed.

Ailsa

My dear Ailsa,

These are the six characteristics of a genuine *compañera*:

1. A genuine *compañera* breaks open her life and her bread with another.

2. A genuine *compañera* trusts her companion to hold her bread with the most delicate and sensitive hands.

3. A genuine *compañera* entrusts her feelings in the good times and the bad times, in the thick and the thin—when she's lonely, when she's excited, when she is vulnerable, when her heart is full and when the tide begins to go out. Never trapped in the misgiving that too much has been said.

4. A genuine *compañera* at her best never allows those demons of self-criticism to beat her up and leave her uncertain of her grace and beauty.

5. A genuine *compañera* has a soul as free as the rolling waves of the ocean.

6. A genuine *compañera* takes time to recognise the miracles of life, and break them open for others.

Might I say, I have never met a more genuine and whole-hearted *compañera* than this sunny spirit who arrived from the vast plains of the sheep-filled west of Oz.

For the genuine *compañeros* of life—*deo gratias*.

Antonio, the novice *compañero*.

Tony!

Too much, too much.

Thank you. I think I will print that off and carry it in my wallet, along with other treasures that sustain me.

I just realised it's a great luxury to be typing this. My laptop will be delivered to my sister Amanda at around eleven tomorrow, and I'll then be reduced to the hen-peck typing of the iPhone. I'm also prevaricating because for some silly reason I feel reluctant to 'farewell' you. And I'm not farewelling you! I will write–just that I will be restrained. You will write, and you will be extravagant with words and stories. Do you hear?

Seriously, I know the coming days and weeks may be difficult for you with your Peter's health, and I'm only joking about the instruction to write.

I'm sorry this letter is so scatty.

And I'm sorry for saying sorry again! Message received, *compañero*.

With gratitude.

Ailsa

Good morning Ailsa!

Just been listening to news of possible water restrictions

on the Gascoyne River. Thought—nine months ago I would have ignored this news bulletin and got on with shaving. Now it's like news about my family.

How times change.

Tony

Hello Tony,

Funny how our ears tune in to things. How our priorities shift based on who and what we know. How we come to care about such abstract or remote things through the experience of another. Lovely, somehow, but so serendipitous. All the other things we might care about. All that we might have missed had we not stopped to care for this person.

Sliding doors.

I'm glad we stopped for each other.

A

Tony!

Me again. This time, bearing a gift.

Christmas is, for me, a time of reflection and a time of reading. Peter and I always give each other Christmas books. That's one of the reasons I'm so thrilled when people tell me they are giving *Sinning* as a gift.

This year, though, time and space is the gift. So I'm making myself files to load onto that tiny iPhone screen, for reading and reflecting. And among them, I have a file called 'PiperDoherty'. Our correspondence to date is a tome, Antonio!

I've collected it all, without email addresses, dates, hyperlinks to cat jokes or any other such stuff, and I attach it here. I wanted to go back over our conversation, because much of it has been at such a pace. Frantic, almost. Trying to cram worlds of ideas in, to catch up on missed years. There are questions that went unanswered and stories that need deeper consideration. There are details that were skipped over, and delights that went unremarked. And so I thought I would take you with me to Ubud, and on the days when a dose of Doherty is required, I will just meander through an email.

So here is a copy for you. This attachment is your Christmas gift. Please imagine it comes wrapped in stiff brown paper. I like that best. Always have. Then it's tied with red silk ribbon. Not my favourite deep crimson blood red, but the hot poinsettia red of the season. There is a hand-cut card, and written on the underside is the word *Compañero*.

Pull the ribbon. Enjoy the slippery satiny silkiness of it as it falls away. Rip the paper. It's thick. Heavy. It's lovely to tear it. Don't wait.

There is your gift. A scroll. Roll it down. You will need to hold it with both hands to keep it still–that's a good reminder for anyone when dealing with me at any time.

Inhale. Read. It's the gift we've already given each other. To me it is a wonder, and as ever, I am grateful.

Feliz Navidad. Buon Natale. Peace.

At this time of year, a birth is celebrated, not a death.

With love,

Ailsa x

DEAR READER,

There's something I haven't told you, and I must, to honour two good men.

My husband Peter died on 18 May 2014. That was the reason for putting aside all my writing projects for more than a year. I was navigating grief. I was a widow. I suppose I still am. I'm trying to learn what it means to be without the person with whom I spent half my life, the person around whom I shaped my days.

When Tony lost his brother Peter, I hope I was a support for him. I tried to write letters that would comfort, divert and amuse. Our friendship was only a year old then, and I was uncertain about how much I should ask or offer— particularly at a distance.

After my Peter died, our friendship was not new. We had known each other for two years by then. Sometimes it seemed like two lifetimes! Tony was a stalwart. He was a quiet, reassuring presence on the day of Peter's funeral. He wrote to me in the time that followed, of course. But he also spoke with me on the phone almost every day afterwards, sometimes waiting for minutes on end for me to be able to form words. Whether he heard sobs, fury or just sullen resentment, he stuck it out. He ministered to his friend. And he never once pressured me to return to writing–or to our project.

When I did go back to our letters, I was reminded of what I had lost. All those days spent hiking the hills near our shack ended with the smell of wood-smoke from Peter's fires, as I'd walk up the driveway. Behind the description of that day spent prepping for the dinner party, there was Peter–going out into the blasting heat to bring home a table for our feast, breaking up bags of ice, choosing music. Ordinary things. Our life, as it was . . .

Of course we didn't throw dinners like that often, but we did love to break bread with friends, whether in the bush or at home. He was nervous before guests arrived, which bemused me, because his stories were always engaging, his hosting attentive and his curiosity boundless. It would have been easy for people to look at Peter's knees-up imperson- ation of the Irish dancer, Michael Flatley, and to believe he was a full-time extrovert party animal.

But that wasn't so. He was complex and a conundrum, as we all are, and I'm not going to be able to write anything that could approach the sum of that good man I loved for his decency and humour; admired for his talent and dedi- cation to craft; and honoured for his constant striving to be better. Peter and I were together for over 27 years. I can barely remember who I was before him—I had been his 'other half' for more than half of my life when he died.

It was sudden. A brain haemorrhage. He was in our bed in our home, learning lines for a role he was to film the following week. I was in Sydney. I'd gone north for a speaking job about my book. Routine stuff for both of us. We were often apart for work we loved. We had texted, sent photos and chatted in the preceding days, but on the Sunday, I couldn't raise him. I told myself it was nothing, that he often didn't hear his mobile or left it behind. But eventually, I panicked and asked our neighbour, a doctor, to go into the house and check. I will never forget what he said when he called me back.

'Oh, Ailsa. I'm so sorry.'

Five words to change your life.

The crazy thing is that I never thought Peter would die before me, despite the fact that he was fifteen years older. I've been over-anxious about others I love–I'm even more so now–but I always thought of Peter as permanent. The rock. I thought I would go first. I was the one who made a will and took out insurance when we travelled. But there was no insuring against that loss.

I still can't fathom his death. The last time I looked into his eyes, when he dropped me at the airport, he shooed me off. 'Go on,' he said. 'Go quickly so you can come back quickly. You know I love you.' All was on the up. We were making plans for changes to our lives. Our eyes were on the future in a way they hadn't been for years. And then he was gone.

He died alone. I can't bear that.

I know everyone dies alone, and I know there's nothing I could have done. I know I don't keep planes in the air, or hearts beating. Not even Pete's. But still . . .

I should have been there. I think of being with my mother

and stroking her hair as she lay dying, and I've listened as Tony tells me how he massaged his brother's feet, and I ache. I wish I could have stroked Peter's forehead or whispered something to help him let go. But his was not that kind of death, I was told.

People said he would never have known; that it was instant; that he would not have wanted me to see him die. Friends sat with me, telling stories and listening to mine, helping me make sense. They bathed me when I was unwell and fed me–body and soul. I wasn't easy. I held my emotions in because I felt I had no right to tears–I was here and alive, when Peter was not. My job was to get on with it; to do the work of a widow.

Amid the mountain of paperwork and endless dealings with legalities and utilities, one task became a lifeline. Every day, I tended the flowers people sent. I'd start before dawn, trimming stems and re-filling vases. Some say sending flowers is a waste because they don't last–but caring for them taught me, over and over because I am slow to learn, that even beautiful things must die.

When they arrived, brought to my door by a succession of sheepish blokes in dented delivery vans, I'd imagine they were a gift from Peter, like the irises he would bring back from the corner shops. I kept them alive as long as I could, clipped and snipped them as they withered and died, ministering to them as I had not been able to do for Pete. And then, I let them go. I had no choice.

The flowers gave me a ritual to shape my days in the first months. They were teachers. Rituals help, when words and people can't. They express the inexpressible.

Of course I had formal rituals in the aftermath. The funeral service was scripted and directed by me to the last second. The wake was a reconstruction of the country hall near our shack, and the afternoon tea at the local agricultural show. Friends and family helped me to make those remembrances perfect for him. It was something I could do, when I had not been able to care for his body because it was in the hands of the coroner. I'd had no chance to farewell his ears, his toes, his familiar eyebrows.

One ritual I remember vividly was a humble, handmade one.

My sister Alanna had stayed with me in the house from the first night, but she had to return to Perth the day after the funeral. She insisted someone be with me when she left, knowing another goodbye might prove too much. I told her not to be silly, but she held firm. She's wise, my sis. She contacted Tony, who had not yet returned to Sydney, and asked him to come. My chest hurt as the front gate clicked behind her. Tony and I waved her off and then he asked what I would like to do.

'Tea,' I said, as I would countless times each day for months to come. We sipped it in silence, in wintry afternoon sun. Then he asked again what I would like to do. I didn't know.

'Tell me the story of this house,' he said. 'Tell me the history of you two, and your home.'

So we walked up the hall to the front room, in which Peter and I had slept for our entire marriage, the room in which he had died, and I began to talk: about where we'd bought each painting; the chest of drawers that had belonged to his favourite glamorous aunt; the photos of our little wedding-present pup; the picture of our shack and how we'd found it, 25 years earlier . . .

We moved into the next room, which had been Peter's 'snug', made over by Alanna into a bedroom for me, because I couldn't bear to return to our room. I told how Peter would sit through the night watching the Tour de France in that

room, and how we'd rearrange the furniture for Wimble-
don. How he would learn his lines there, escape from heat
there, and chuckle at late night talk shows as I lay in our
room reading . . .

Next, the bathroom, where I pointed out the artworks
by Alanna, and explained where we'd found the clawfoot
tub and how we'd laughed when the architect who was
planning our renovations said we were impossible because
I wanted a tree-house and Pete wanted a cave . . .

We climbed the stairs to my study where there was a
banner Peter had made, and I recalled how he'd drawn
up political signs for the back of his car, and how he once
sat at a polling booth in our conservative electorate with
a placard about the plight of refugees, and how people
eyed him suspiciously and then ended up being charmed
by him and chatting. I got out the albums and we looked at
wedding shots and travel snaps and show photos . . .

Suddenly, I was overwhelmed. It had been a tsunami of
telling, and I'm sure Tony was exhausted. Listening is work.
We went downstairs and had more tea. Then Tony asked,
'Now what?'

'I'd like you to pray with me,' I said.

I have no idea where it came from, but it was a deep need, and Tony didn't blink. We sat on either side of the coffee table. I lit my meditation candle, and we were silent a while. Then I picked up the Buddhist prayer that friends were saying for Peter, and we read it together. It had a line I loved–'Peter has taken the great leap.' I wanted to believe he had leapt, and not fallen or been cut down.

Then I said I wanted to say the Our Father. Again, I've no idea why. But we said those words, then Tony suggested we also say the Hail Mary, and so we did.

He asked if he might offer words of thanks for Peter's life, speaking about the feeling of the house, and of the man he had met at dinner and again, at a meal in Sydney the previous Christmas. He talked of the colour in our home, and of what Peter and I had created together. And then he fell silent, and I spoke. Things I had not been able to say.

I asked Pete's forgiveness for not having been with him at the end. I said how I couldn't locate him in the house, and how it felt like he had gone so fast, so fast. I apologised for not having been able to care for his body after he died, and I told him how much I wished that his way was safe and clear. Whatever it had been. To wherever he had gone.

Tony and I sat a little longer in silence, then I extinguished the candle, and we made tea. Finally I asked why he thought I'd wanted to say the Lord's Prayer.

'Because it's the prayer of your childhood, from a time when everything was safe.'

Childhood. Safety. Some god who could make everything all right.

I so wanted to believe in Tony's God, but I couldn't. I was angry at the idea of a god who could take Peter too soon and too suddenly–even though I wanted any god for comfort. Perverse creature.

But there was comfort, even when I wouldn't see it– Tony, my stalwart brothers, sisters and father, Pete's loyal tribe, and my many extraordinary friends–to step me through the shadow of Peter's death. They were blessings, confirming that grace waits to be found, if we will just look. Sometimes it's hard–but kindness always offset despair when I lifted my eyes. We can't take away or undo pain, but we can sit with people, hear their stories, walk with them, bake bread, drop soup, or make tea. We can bear witness and be human. In that, there is grace.

And in that everyday grace, I gradually came home. It

has taken me a long time to reach the point where I can say, without feeling guilty, that I want to live–understanding deep in my bones that living means losing. There is no way around it. We must accept that there will be loss. But there are trees and birds, trails to walk and water to heal, and there is life-giving sun. With every breath, I want to be in it.

Ailsa

POSTSCRIPT

These days Ailsa lives in Sydney, and rides ferries to the city. When she pulls in to Circular Quay, there is the Opera House, and beside it, the Chinese restaurant where she met her new-but-familiar friend. She walks along harbour trails and sandstone cliffs. She is learning to swim! There is a seahorse colony near her home, and the resilience of those creatures, with their skeletons on the outside, inspires her. She is writing again. And speaking, teaching, convening, narrating audiobooks . . .

She is coming home.

Tony has undergone a significant shift in his daily work. From being in charge of two Sydney parishes, he has moved to what is described in the trade as 'lesser duties'. He likes to call them 'better duties'. Now free of the demanding administration of a large Catholic community, he lives privately, giving him more space for his preferred pastoral work of being with people as they find meaning in the ups and downs of their life journey–marriages, funerals, counselling–as well as assisting at Sunday Mass in the wider Sydney Church. More time for writing too, and for making sense of his own most fortunate life. Funny thing– less time for golf but more time for cooking.

The conversation between the Shanachie and the Priest hasn't stopped. Nor has the laughter. Their friendship remains a surprise and support for both of them–even when they are arguing, which they still do. Often! They have not stopped hunting for that elusive Copper to complete their village . . .

ACKNOWLEDGEMENTS

Thank you. *Gracias* . . .

To our first readers, Keith Robinson and Vicki Hastrich. Without your encouragement we might never have felt emboldened to proceed.

To Jane Palfreyman. Your 'yes' was a gift wrapped in red ribbon. We've been enriched by your insight, generosity, wisdom and laughter.

To the Allen & Unwin family, and in particular to Genevieve Buzo, whose close attention has supported us so beautifully. Also to Romina Panetta, whose visuals delighted us, and to Julia Cain, who made us look again!

To James Laurie. You're the business!

Ailsa's three-week residency at Bundanon was invaluable at a time when the idea of a book seemed impossible. An earlier week at Varuna gave us both the opportunity to advance our thinking.

From Ailsa

Thank you to my remarkable 'village' of friends for guiding me home through the dark. To my Sydney writing chums, for conversations that sustained my energy for work, and a huzzah to Caroline Baum for title inspiration.

From Tony

For a lifetime of friends—believers and unbelievers—who have shared their stories and their profound life experiences with me over many years, I am grateful. You have shaped me with your questions, your insights and your conversation, towards a richer understanding of myself and my ministry.

ABOUT THE AUTHORS

WENDY MCDOUGALL

Ailsa Piper is a storyteller and walker. She has worked as a writer, director, actor, teacher, speaker and broadcaster.

One writing highlight was being named co-winner of the Patrick White Playwrights' Award for her script *Small Mercies* in 2001. Another came in 2012 with the publication of her first book, *Sinning Across Spain*, the story of her 1300-kilometre walk along a less-travelled pilgrim trail. She also wrote and performed an episode of ABC Radio's *Poetica* about the poetry that inspired her journey. In the same year, she co-adapted a version of Webster's *The Duchess of Malfi* for Bell Shakespeare.

Ailsa has judged the NSW and Victorian Premiers' Literary Awards seven times, and regularly contributes articles to magazines and newspapers. An accomplished interviewer and moderator, she also performs *Wordwalks* –solo performances celebrating poetry, walking and the spirit of place.

Monsignor Tony Doherty has worked as a priest and educator in Sydney for over fifty years. His most recent ministry was to the parishes of Rose Bay and Dover Heights for twelve years.

During five decades of pastoral work as a Catholic priest, he has been a hospital chaplain, adult educator and writer. He has designed strategies for renewing parishes, and contributed to radio and television, including the two TV series *Echo of a Distant Drum* (the story of the Irish in Australia) and the award-winning *Brides of Christ*.

In 1995 he coordinated the visit of Pope John Paul II to Sydney for the special recognition of Saint Mary MacKillop. While Dean of St Mary's Cathedral he led a conservation team in finishing the original 1865 design, which saw the southern spires completed at last.

He is a frequent writer and commentator on religious and wider community issues, and in 2012 received an Order of Australia.